New Methods for the Arbitrage Pricing Theory and the Present Value Model

New Methods for the Arbitrage Pricing Theory and the Present Value Model

Jianping Mei

New York University, USA

World Scientific
Singapore • New Jersey • London • Hong Kong

332.645
M49n

Published by

World Scientific Publishing Co. Pte. Ltd.

P O Box 128, Farrer Road, Singapore 9128

USA office: Suite 1B, 1060 Main Street, River Edge, NJ 07661

UK office: 73 Lynton Mead, Totteridge, London N20 8DH

NEW METHODS FOR THE ARBITRAGE PRICING THEORY
AND THE PRESENT VALUE MODEL

ISBN: 981-02-1839-7

Printed in Singapore by Utopia Press.

ACKNOWLEDGEMENT

It is a great pleasure for me to express my gratitude to the following persons and institutions for the publication of my dissertation, presented to the faculty of Princeton University for the Ph.D. degree in Economics in 1990.

My first and foremost thanks go to Professors John Campbell (committee Chairman), Glen Donaldson, Burton Malkiel and Richard Quandt. They have provided me with encouragement, inspiration, and intellectual challenges during my four-year study at Princeton. I also want to thank Professor Gregory Chow, who helped me to come to Princeton and made it possible for me to pursue this study.

I am grateful to the Graduate School of Princeton University and the John M. Olin Foundation for Study of Economic Organization and Public Policy for their generous financial support in the last four years.

I also want express my gratitude to Dean Zheng Shaolian of Fudan Business School and Dr. K.K. Phua of World Scientific Publishing Co Pte Ltd, whose encouragement made this publication possible. It has also been a pleasure for me to work with my editor, Miss Gillian Chee.

Finally, I want to dedicate my dissertation to my parents Yuqin Mei and Jiazhen Peng, My mother-in-law Naicheng Sheng, my wife Wei and my daughter Grayce for their warm support.

Jianping Mei

New York University

April 1994

CONTENTS

ABSTRACT

This dissertation consists of two essays on developing new methods for testing the Arbitrage Pricing Theory (APT) and the Present Value Model (PVM), and one essay on correcting heteroskedasticity and cross-sectional correlation in panel study by using the Newey-West Adjustment Matrix.

In the first essay, I develop an autoregressive method for testing the APT. Unlike methods currently being used in the literature, this method does not require prior estimation of factor loadings and risk premia. The new methodology is based on the observation that past returns of an asset carry information about its exposure to systematic risks and thus can be used to construct *ex post* risk adjustments for the asset via a cross-sectional autoregressive model. I derive several testable implications of the APT and drop a crucial assumption that factor risk premia are constant. The approach is robust to changes in factor loadings in some cases. I find little evidence that firm size contribute additional explanatory power to that of factor loadings in the APT model.

The second essay studies the rational expectations present value model with variable expected returns. I develop an econometric method with which (i) to test a general model of expected returns and (ii) to test a linearalized version of the present value model. I find that share dividend-price ratios carry information about the structure of future dividend growth. I also find that the rejection of the present value model is dependent upon the variability of expected returns.

The third essay is an outcome of joint work with Whitney Newey. We show that the Newey-West adjustment matrix can be very useful for correcting heteroskedasticity and cross-sectional correlation in panel studies. We apply that adjustment procedure to the vector autoregression model of Holtz-Eakin, Newey and Rosen and develop a chi-square test to determine the number of pervasive economic factors in an approximate factor model. Our empirical results suggest there are at least seven factors in the economy that affect returns of securities listed on the New York Stock Exchange from 1987-1988.

Do We Have to Know Betas?
An Autoregressive Method for Testing the APT*

* I would like to thank Douglas Holtz-Eakin, who graciously provided me with the program for autoregression. I am also grateful to Gordon Bodnar, Stephen Brown, Gregory Chow, Dexter Chu, Angus Deaton, Glen Donaldson, Bill Gentry, Daniel Hardy, Albert Margolis, Whitney Newey and Harvey Rosen for helpful comments. This research is supported by the John M. Olin Foundation for Study of Economic Organization and Public Policy.

I. Introduction

A major difficulty encountered by empirical financial economists is that some key variables and parameters are not observable in models of the equilibrium relationship between risk and return. Although empirical study of the Arbitrage Pricing Theory (APT) has been going on for a decade now, estimation methods for unobservable betas and risk premia remain a focus of current research.

The original method of testing the APT model developed by Roll and Ross (1980) is first to estimate betas through factor analysis. Then the estimated betas are used as data to perform a cross-sectional regression to obtain estimates of risk premia. This approach is similar to the two-step procedure developed by Fama and MacBeth (1973) in their famous study of the Capital Asset Pricing Model (CAPM).

The core of Roll and Ross' methodology, which is the two-step approach of factor analysis plus regression, has been employed in many subsequent studies, although several improvements have been made to avoid some of the pitfalls in their work. Chen (1983) uses a procedure that does not require the splitting of the universe of securities into many small subgroups. Lehmann and Modest (1985) apply an EM algorithm to the maximum likelihood factor analysis to estimate betas. A revised version of the two-step approach is used to construct test statistics. Another variant of the two-step approach is the asymptotic principle components technique proposed by Connor and Korajczyk (1988).

The two-step approach has long been recognized to be subject to an errors-in-variables problem. Various techniques have been tried to solve the problem. Brown and Weinstein (1983) employ an iterative procedure to obtain the factors and loadings from a first order condition for maximizing a likelihood function.[1] Unfortunately, the procedure does not guarantee convergence and the results are dependent on the starting values used for the iteration. Jobson (1982) develops a multivariate linear regression test of the APT model, which uses observable "mimicking" portfolios to replace the unobservable factors. His insight is that a set of K well diversified portfolios carries enough information about the factors in the market, and thus can be used as substitutes for the unobservable factors. But his assumption that the K portfolios have no idiosyncratic risks

---

[1] Gibbons (1982) has applied a similar procedure to the study of the CAPM.

4

makes his approach difficult to accept and implement in practice. Burmeister and McElroy (1988) drop this assumption by estimating the Jobson equation system with a iterated nonlinear three-stage-least-square (ITNL3SLS) procedure. But the procedure may suffer from the same pitfall as Brown and Weinstein's.

Another line of research in the literature is represented by the works of Gibbons and Ferson (1985) and Campbell (1987), which employ latent-variable models. Although their approach drops the assumption of constant risk premia and is easy to apply in practice, they pay a cost of assuming an model of conditional expectations.

In this paper, an autoregressive approach is developed to test the APT model. The basic idea is that historical returns of an asset contain information about its exposure to systematic risks in the market and can be utilized to mimic the unobservable factor loadings. The central implication of the APT is that it imposes restrictions on coefficients of a cross-sectional autoregressive models. These restrictions are testable by a *linear* three-stage-least-square (3SLS) procedure.

The autoregressive approach has other benefits as well. This paper successfully drops a crucial assumption often made in the APT literature, namely, that the factor premia are constant over time.[2] This generalization, together with the autoregressive model, opens some new possibilities for studying models of variable expected returns, which might hold the key to the understanding of many financial anomalies, such as the mean reversion phenomenon and the excess volatility puzzle. See Mei (1989) for a preliminary study of the present value model with variable expected returns.

Since a linear combination of historical returns is used for making risk adjustments, this method does not need to estimate betas for hypothesis testing. Thus the problem of errors-in-variables is completely eliminated. As a result, we have many fewer parameters which need estimation. With a large panel data set and the relatively small number of parameters in the model, we should feel more comfortable applying asymptotic distribution theory. Although the approach is similar in spirit to that of Jobson, it does not require any stringent assumptions. In comparison with many previous computationally demanding studies, this

---

[2] This assumption is used in Roll and Ross to calculate mean asset returns and their variance-covariance matrix.

method is much simpler and more intuitive.

The paper will be organized as follows: Section II illustrates the main idea of the paper using a simple one-factor model. Section III offers a complete study of some testable implications of the APT for the autoregressive model. Section IV describes the data and presents empirical results. Section V discusses the robustness of our study to changes in betas. Section VI concludes.

II. The Example of a One-factor Model

Assume we observe returns in two different periods on a group of securities, which are generated by the following model:

$$R_{it} = \alpha_{it} + f_t\, \beta_i + \varepsilon_{it} \qquad\qquad i = 1,...,N; \qquad t = 1,2 \qquad (1)$$

where

R_{it} is return on asset i in period t ;

f_t is an unobservable random factor;

β_i is the factor loading associated with f_t, which is time invariant;

$\varepsilon_t = (\varepsilon_{1t},..., \varepsilon_{Nt})'$ represent an idiosyncratic risk.

We assume that $\{\varepsilon_{it}, t=1,2\}$ are a pair of independently distributed (i.i.d) random vectors with

$$E(\varepsilon_t) = 0; \quad E(f_t) = 0; \qquad E(\varepsilon_t | f_t) = 0 \ \text{ and } \ Cov(\varepsilon_t) = D.$$

where D is a diagonal matrix.

In an efficient economy with no arbitrage opportunities, we should have:

$$\alpha_{it} = R_t + \lambda_t\, \beta_i. \qquad\qquad (2)$$

where

R_t is the risk free rate of return;

λ_t is the factor premium associated with f_t.

Substituting (2) into (1), we obtain:

$$R_{it} = R_t + (f_t + \lambda_t)\, \beta_i + \varepsilon_{it} \qquad\qquad i = 1,...,N; \qquad t = 1,2 \qquad (3)$$

Note that the economy here is driven by a systematic shock, while the return structure is determined by factor loading β_i and firm specific shocks. If we can obtain information on β_i, then using the information in equation (3), we will be able to estimate (3) *through a cross-sectional regression* and study its implications. To get information on β_i, the traditional approach is to regress R_{it} on some market indexes, using time series data, and get an estimate of β_i. Our approach is different . We notice that past returns carry information about β_i. If we can solve for β_i in terms of past returns and some parameters which are constant across firms, we can use (3) and do an autoregression analysis. So we ask the following question: How much *cross-sectional* variation of R_{i2} can be explained by past return R_{i1}, if R_{i1} carries information about β_i ? To put it in a regression context , can we obtain a "useful " regression if we regress R_{i2} on R_{i1}?

$$R_{i2} = \psi_0 + \psi_1 R_{i1} + \eta_i , \qquad i=1, ... , N. \quad (4)$$

The answer is yes. Denoting $R_{.1}$ (the same for $R_{.2}$, $\beta.$ and $\varepsilon_{.t}$) as a random variable whose N realizations (R_{11} , R_{21} , ... , R_{N1})' determine the structure of returns in time period 1, let us first calculate the correlation coefficient between the left-hand-side(LHS) and right-hand-side(RHS) variable, $R_{.2}$ and $R_{.1}$ *across firms, conditional on the two realization of f_t, f_1 and f_2*. We should point out here that when we study the variation of returns across firms at any given time, the random variation comes from the difference in β_i and ε_{it} across firms. [3]

$$\rho(R_{.2},R_{.1}|f_t,t=1,2) = \frac{(f_2+\lambda_2)(f_1+\lambda_1)\mathrm{var}(\beta.)}{\sqrt{(f_2+\lambda_2)^2\mathrm{var}(\beta.)+\mathrm{var}(\varepsilon_{.2})}\sqrt{(f_1+\lambda_1)^2\mathrm{var}(\beta.)+\mathrm{var}(\varepsilon_{.1})}} \quad (5)$$

in which var($\beta.$) is the variation of β_i across firms, and var($\varepsilon_{.t}$) is the marginal variance of ε_{it} across firms given time period t=1,2. Here we assume that the random variables $\beta.$ and $\varepsilon_{.t}$ are uncorrelated.

The sample conditional correlation coefficient is calculated by:

$$\hat{\rho}(R_{.2},R_{.1}|f_t,t=1,2) = \frac{\sum_{i=1}^{N}(R_{i2}-\bar{R}_2)(R_{i1}-\bar{R}_1)/N}{\sqrt{\sum_{i=1}^{N}(R_{i2}-\bar{R}_2)^2/N}\sqrt{\sum_{i=1}^{N}(R_{i1}-\bar{R}_1)^2/N}} \quad (6)$$

where $\bar{R}_1$ and $\bar{R}_2$ are the cross-sectional mean of R_{i1} and R_{i2}. We can clearly see from (5) and (6) that the correlation coefficient between $R_{.2}$ and $R_{.1}$ *across firms* is different from the correlation coefficient between $R_{i,t}$ and $R_{i,t-1}$ *over time for a given i*.

---

[3] This correlation should be distinguished from the correlation between R_{i2} on R_{i1} *over time* , *conditional on a given i* . In that case, the random variables are f_t and ε_{it}, which change over time. We know the correlation coefficient should be close to zero, implying that future return can not be predicted by past return.

It is obvious that the correlation coefficient (5) is a function of f_1 and f_2. It can be either positive or negative, depending on the realization of f_1 and f_2. It also depends on how noisy are the firm specific shocks and how much variation there is in the factor loadings across firms. Since we do not know f_2 before time 2, equation (5) will not help us in picking securities *in period 1* that could give us abnormal return *in period 2. This implies future returns are still unpredictable.*

Because the correlation coefficient will generally be non-zero, we will get a non-zero ψ_1 if we estimate regression (4). In what follows, we will formally derive equation (4) and the constraints imposed on ψ_0 and ψ_1 by equation (3).

Take equation (3) for time period 1, to extract information about β_i from R_{i1}, we solve for β_i in terms of R_{i1}:

$$\beta_i = \frac{R_{i1} - R_1 - \varepsilon_{i1}}{f_1 + \lambda_1}. \tag{7}$$

Although f_1, λ_1, R_1 and ε_{i1} are not observable, we note f_1, λ_1 and R_1 are constant across firms and the error term, ε_{i1}, has desirable properties. Substituting (7) into (3) for time period 2, we obtain:

$$R_{i2} = R_2 + (f_2 + \lambda_2)\frac{R_{i1} - R_1 - \varepsilon_{i1}}{f_1 + \lambda_1} + \varepsilon_{i2}. \tag{8}$$

Collecting terms, we have:

$$R_{i2} = R_2 - \frac{f_2 + \lambda_2}{f_1 + \lambda_1} R_1 + \frac{f_2 + \lambda_2}{f_1 + \lambda_1} R_{i1} + \varepsilon_{i2} - \frac{f_2 + \lambda_2}{f_1 + \lambda_1} \varepsilon_{i1}. \quad i=1,\cdots,N. \tag{9}$$

Combining (9) with (4), we can see that :

$$\psi_0 = R_2 - \frac{f_2 + \lambda_2}{f_1 + \lambda_1} R_1; \quad \psi_1 = \frac{f_2 + \lambda_2}{f_1 + \lambda_1}; \quad \eta_i = \varepsilon_{i2} - \frac{f_2 + \lambda_2}{f_1 + \lambda_1} \varepsilon_{i1}. \tag{10}$$

where ψ_0 and ψ_1 are constant across firms. If $R_1 = R_2 = R$, then we can see the restriction imposed on ψ_0 and ψ_1 of (4) by equation (3) is :

$$\psi_0 / R + \psi_1 = 1 \tag{11}$$

Thus the one-factor model (3) can be tested by running a *cross-sectional* autoregression (4) in time period 2 and testing the restriction (11). We will show later that it is also possible to test the linear pricing relationship of (2) against some other alternatives and also to test whether the factor, f_t, is "priced" in this framework.

It is obvious from (10), that the error term in (4) is uncorrelated across firms and has a mean of zero. Except for the fact that R_{i1} is correlated with the error term, equation (4) is a standard linear regression model. If we can find instruments for R_{i1}, then (4) can be estimated by an instrumental variables regression, and (11) can be tested using a Wald test.

The choice of instruments for R_{i1} can be crucial, since it affects estimation efficiency in a small sample. If we observe asset returns in a third period, R_{i0}, and R_{i0} satisfies (3), then R_{i0} can be used as an instrument for R_{i1}. Other variables which are known at the beginning of time 1 and carry information about asset's risk features such as the security's P/E ratio, size, or dividend yield, also qualify as potential instruments.

It is worth noting here that although there always exists an *ex post* efficient benchmark portfolio by which an ex post beta can be defined and to make the linear relationship hold, that "benchmark portfolio" will not necessarily be on the *ex ante* efficient portfolio frontier. In other words, the ex post beta may not be written as a linear function of the true beta. Thus, the regression of asset returns on the *ex post* beta (or on lagged returns) will generally not give error terms that are uncorrelated, which is assumed in the linear factor model of (1). This correlation of errors will bias the estimates of regression coefficients and their covariance matrix and thus may lead to a rejection of the model. So the tests here are joint tests of the linear pricing relationship and the linear factor model of (1), either the violation of the linear pricing relationship or the misspecification of the linear factor model will cause a statistical rejection.

Although the above discussion deals only with (t=1,2), this methodology applies to multi-time periods as well. The economic interpretation of regression (4) is that the realized return structure of today can be partly explained *ex post* by that of yesterday, given that we observe the realization of today and yesterday's returns (Hence, f_t and f_{t-1} become fixed numbers.). But we can not use (4) to predict future returns, since ψ_1 is time-varying and dependent on the realization of future f_t.

III. Test of the Arbitrage Pricing Theory

In Section II, we have demonstrated that a one-factor APT model (3) can be transformed to a one-lag autoregressive model (4), by using information about β_i conveyed in past returns. In what follows, we extend this approach to a multi-factor APT model. We will derive a generalization of (4) and discuss several constraints imposed on its coefficients by the APT model. The only difference multiple factors make is that more lags of past returns are now needed to extract information about the betas.

Assume that capital markets are perfectly competitive and frictionless. Investors believe that asset returns are generated by the following K-factor model:

$$R_{it} = \alpha_{i,t} + f_{1t}\,\beta_{i1} + \dots + f_{Kt}\,\beta_{iK} + \varepsilon_{it} \qquad i = 1,\dots,N; \qquad t = 1,\dots,T. \qquad (12)$$

where

$\alpha_{i,t}$ is the expected return on asset i conditional on
information set I_t known at the beginning of period t.

$f_t{}' = (f_{1t},\dots,f_{Kt})$ is a vector of unobservable random factors with
time-varying distributions;

$(\beta_{i1},\dots,\beta_{iK})$ is a vector of factor loadings which are time invariant; and

ε_{it} represents an idiosyncratic risk specific to asset i;

We assume that $\{\varepsilon_{it}, t=1,\dots,T\}$ are a series of independently distributed random vectors with

$$E(\varepsilon_t) = 0; \quad E(f_t) = 0; \quad Cov(f_t, f_t) = \Lambda_t; \quad E(\varepsilon_t \mid f_t) = 0 \text{ and } Cov(\varepsilon_t) = D_t.$$

where Λ_t and D_t are diagonal matrices. We assume f_t are independent over time.

In a well diversified capital market with no arbitrage opportunities, the equilibrium expected return is given by:

$$\alpha_{i,t} = \lambda_{0t} + \lambda_{1t}\,\beta_{i1} + \dots + \lambda_{Kt}\,\beta_{iK}, \qquad (13)$$

where $(\lambda_{1t},\dots, \lambda_{Kt})$ is a vector of risk premia corresponding to
the risk factors $(f_{1t},\dots,f_{Kt})$; and
λ_{0t} is the return on a riskless (or "zero beta") asset.

Combining (12) and (13) and denoting $s_t' = (s_{1t},...,s_{Kt}) = (f_{1t},...,f_{Kt}) + (\lambda_{1t},..., \lambda_{Kt})$ and $\beta_i' = (\beta_{i1},..., \beta_{iK})$, we obtain,

$$R_{i,t} = \lambda_{0t} + s_t' \beta_i + \varepsilon_{i,t} . \qquad\qquad i=1,..., N; \ t=1,...,T. \qquad (14)$$

To extract information about β_i from historical return data $R_{i,s}$ (s<t), we take equation (14) for asset i from time period t-1 to t-K, and "stack" them on top of one another and move λ_{0t} and $\varepsilon_{i,t}$ to the other side, and denote :

$$S_t = \begin{bmatrix} s_{1,t-1} & \cdots & s_{K,t-1} \\ \vdots & \vdots & \vdots \\ s_{1,t-K} & \cdots & s_{K,t-K} \end{bmatrix} \qquad \Pi_{it} = \begin{bmatrix} R_{i,t-1} - \lambda_{0,t-1} - \varepsilon_{i,t-1} \\ \vdots \\ R_{i,t-K} - \lambda_{0,t-K} - \varepsilon_{i,t-K} \end{bmatrix}$$

S_t is a KxK matrix and Π_{it} is a Kx1 matrix. Thus, we have,

$$S_t \beta_i = \Pi_{it} . \qquad\qquad (15)$$

Assume there are no redundant factors in the model so that S is non-singular. We solve for β_i,

$$\beta_i = S_t^{-1} \Pi_{it} ,$$

and substituting it into (15) for time period t, we have:

$$R_{i,t} = \lambda_{0t} + s_t' S_t^{-1} \Pi_{it} + \varepsilon_{i,t} . \qquad\qquad i=1,..., N, \ t=K+1,...,T. \qquad (16)$$

Collecting terms, and defining $\psi_t' = (\psi_{1t},..., \psi_{Kt}) = s_t' S_t^{-1}$, we have,

$$R_{i,t} = \psi_{0t} + \sum_{j=1}^{K} \psi_{jt} R_{i,t-j} + \eta_{i,t} . \qquad i=1,...,N; \ t=K+1,...,T. \qquad (17)$$

where:

$$\psi_{0,t} = \lambda_{0t} - \sum_{j=1}^{K} \psi_{jt} \lambda_{0,t-j} \qquad \eta_{i,t} = \varepsilon_{it} - \sum_{j=1}^{K} \psi_{jt} \varepsilon_{i,t-j} . \qquad t=K+1,...,T. \qquad (18)$$

Notice that the coefficients of equation (17) are independent of any non-singular transformation of the beta matrix. Suppose the order of $\beta_i' = (\beta_{i1},..., \beta_{iK})$ is rearranged and the scale of β_{ij} adjusted. Then β_i will be replaced by $G \beta_i$ and

s_t will be replaced by $G'^{-1}s_t$ (thus, S_t will be replaced by $S_t\,G^{-1}$), because the return structure is not affected by such a transformation. Since $s_t'S_t{}^{-1}$ is replaced by $s_t'G^{-1}\,(S_t\,G^{-1})^{-1}$, which equals $s_t'S_t{}^{-1}$, we obtain an important property of equation (17). That is the parameters of (17) do not depend on any specific scale and order chosen for the factors(or loadings), i.e., they are invariant with respect to the normalization of the factors.

Since the returns on all securities must satisfy (17), if we split the universe of securities into two or more subgroups and estimate equation (17) separately on the two subgroups:

$$R_{i,t} = \psi_{0t} + \sum_{j=1}^{K} \psi_{jt}\,R_{i,t-j} + \eta_{i,t}\,. \qquad i=1,...,N; \quad t=K+1,...,T.$$

$$R_{i,t} = \omega_{0t} + \sum_{j=1}^{K} \omega_{jt}\,R_{i,t-j} + \eta_{i,t}\,. \qquad i=1,...,N; \quad t=K+1,...,T.$$

(19)

we should not be able to reject :

$$H_0: \quad \psi_{jt} = \omega_{jt}. \qquad\qquad j=0,...,K; \ t=K+1,...,T. \qquad (20)$$

We shall call this test the "test of identity of factors across groups of securities". This test should be more revealing than the test used by Roll and Ross. They were only able to test the intercepts being the same across different subgroups in their cross-sectional regressions, since other coefficients in their regressions are dependent on the transformations mentioned above.

From equations (17) and (18), we can see that the intercept of (17) is restricted to be a function of the risk free rate and lagged coefficients of (17), if the APT is true. If the risk free rate is constant over time, $\lambda_{0t} = \lambda_0$, we must have:

$$\frac{\psi_{0t}}{\lambda_0} + \sum_{j=1}^{K} \psi_{jt} = 1. \qquad\qquad t= K+1,\cdot\cdot,T. \qquad (21)$$

If we observe the risk free rate λ_0, we can use the estimated coefficients of (17) and their variance-covariance matrix to construct a Wald test of hypothesis (21). If λ_0 is not observable, then we can take equation (21) for t=K+1 and solve for λ_0, obtaining,

$$\lambda_0 = \frac{\psi_{0,K+1}}{1 - \sum_{j=1}^{K} \psi_{j,K+1}} \tag{22}$$

Substituting (22) into (21), we obtain,

$$\frac{\psi_{0,t}}{\psi_{0,K+1}} \left(1 - \sum_{j=1}^{K} \psi_{j,K+1}\right) + \sum_{j=1}^{K} \psi_{j,t} = 1. \qquad t=K+2,\cdots,T. \tag{23}$$

Equation (23) defines a nonlinear restriction on the coefficients of equation (17) for each period's regression. A nonlinear Wald test can be constructed to see if the data reject (23).We will call the tests of (21) and (23) the "test of constancy of the risk free rate with λ_0 known and λ_0 unknown".

Next, we will follow Roll and Ross in testing the APT against a specific alternative. If the APT is true, we should not be able to reject H_0: $\pi_t = 0$ in the following regression:

$$R_{i,t} = \psi_{0t} + \sum_{j=1}^{K} \psi_{jt} R_{i,t-j} + \pi_t C_{i,t} + \eta_{i,t}. \qquad i=1,...,N; \quad t=K+1,...,T, \tag{24}$$

where C_{it} represents a firm specific variable such as dividend yield, capitalization or P/E ratio. We will concentrate on C_{it} being the firm's log capitalization in this study. Then rejection of $\pi_t = 0$ indicates the existence of a size anomaly. We will call this the "size effect test".

Since C_{it} may be correlated with η_{it} through its possible correlation with $\varepsilon_{it-j}(j=1,...,K)$, we will use *projected* C_{it} instead of C_{it} in the regression of (24). The projection is made on several variables in the information set I_{t-K}. The intuition of the test is that the projected C_{it} based on information at t-K should not have any explanatory power over the error term η_{it} in equation (17), since it is totally random with respect to time t-K.

Finally, we will study the issue of "factor pricing". It is the central assertion of the APT that only systematic risks should be compensated in the market. And risk averse investors do require a reward for bearing undiversifiable risk. Thus, we should have the factor premia $\lambda_{jt} \neq 0$ at least for some j and some t in equation (13). In what follows, we will formally test the hypothesis H_0: $\lambda_{jt} = 0$ for all j and all t. We will call this test the "test of factor pricing".

Although we can test H_0: $\lambda_{jt} = 0$ by directly testing whether all assets having the same expected return, we will test this hypothesis within the autoregression framework. We notice that the *unconditional* mean of the lagged coefficients, ψ_{jt}, in the autoregression (17) equal zero if the null hypothesis holds. This is because:

$$E(\psi_t) = E\{ E[s_t S_t^{-1} | I_t] \} = E \{ E[f_t S_t^{-1} | I_t] \} = 0, \qquad j=1,...,K. \quad (25)$$

The second equality in (25) follows directly from $\lambda_{jt} = 0$. The third equality comes from the fact that factors f_t are independent over time and have means of zero. Thus the conditional expectation of f_t based on information at the beginning of time t should be zero, making the unconditional expectation of ψ_{jt} zero as well.

Note that ψ_{jt} and ψ_{js} (s > t+K+1) are independent and have the same distribution if f_t are i.i.d. over time. Thus if we can obtain samples of { ψ_{jt} } with the sampling interval at least K+1 apart, we will be able to use the sample means and sample standard errors to calculate a t-statistic and test whether the sample means are significantly different from zero. The rejection of zero means indicates that some λ_{jt} are not zero.

Since we do not observe ψ_{jt}, we will use the *estimated* lagged coefficients from the autoregression to substitute for the true ψ_{jt}. Because ψ_{jt} are estimated by using instrumental variables from K periods back, we need to make the sampling interval of { ψ_{jt} } further apart to make sure that the samples of { ψ_{jt} } are independent. We also need to make sure that the estimation errors of ψ_{jt} are also i.i.d. so that we will be able to use the t-test.

In order to perform the above tests, we need to estimate autoregression (17) by using panel data sets. We rewrite (17) as :

$$\begin{bmatrix} R_{1t} \\ \vdots \\ R_{Nt} \end{bmatrix} = \begin{bmatrix} 1 & R_{1,t-1} & \cdots & R_{1,t-K} \\ \vdots & \vdots & \vdots & \vdots \\ 1 & R_{N,t-1} & \cdots & R_{N,t-K} \end{bmatrix} \begin{bmatrix} \psi_{0,t} \\ \vdots \\ \psi_{K,t} \end{bmatrix} + \begin{bmatrix} \eta_{1,t} \\ \vdots \\ \eta_{N,t} \end{bmatrix} \qquad t=K+1,...,T. \quad (17)$$

We "stack" equations (17) on top of each other by time to make them a system of equations. It looks very much like the classic seemingly unrelated regressions (SUR) system. But here the system is a set of *cross-sectional* regressions for different time periods instead of the conventional set of *time-series* regressions for different individuals. The autoregressors $R_{i,t-j}$

(j=1,...,K) are also correlated with the error term η_{it} through their correlation with $\varepsilon_{it-1},..., \varepsilon_{it-K}$ and there is heteroskedasticity and serial correlation in the error term, η_{it}. Thus equation (17) needs to be estimated by an instrumental variables regression and appropriate adjustments need to be made to take into account the heteroskedasticity and serial correlation.

We employ a 3SLS estimation technique, developed by Holtz-Eakin, Newey and Rosen (1988) to accomplish these tasks. The estimates will be consistent despite the existence of heteroskedasticity and serial correlation. And it is efficient in the class of instrumental variables estimators which use linear combinations of the instrumental variables.

Intuitively, the estimation procedure is quite similar to that of the 3SLS method used in the estimation of simultaneous equations. At the first stage and the second stage, a generalized instrumental variable regression is used to get estimates of (17) for each time period, ignoring the serial correlation and heteroskedasticity. At the third stage, the residuals from the regression of the second stage are used to calculate a White (1980)-type variance-covariance matrix of the error term and a generalized least squares method is used to obtain a more efficient estimate of equation (17) for all time periods.

To test hypotheses (20), (21) and (23), we write the estimated coefficient vector of (17) as γ, the estimated variance-covariance matrix of the vector as Θ, and the vector of deviations from the null hypothesis as H. Then the Wald test statistic is:

$$W = H' [\partial H / \partial \gamma' \, \Theta \, \partial H / \partial \gamma]^{-1} H. \tag{26}$$

Under the null hypothesis, it is distributed as χ^2 with degrees of freedom equal to the number of restrictions imposed on the coefficients.

To test restrictions such as $\pi_t = 0$, we will employ a procedure similar to the Chow test. The strategy is first to estimate the *unrestricted* ($\pi_t \neq 0$)model and the *restricted* ($\pi_t = 0$) model and then calculate the difference in their sum of squared residuals, Q_U and Q_R. If the restriction does not hold, then the difference ($L = Q_R - Q_U$) will be large, indicating a rejection of the hypothesis. It is worth noting here that this procedure can also be used to determine the minimum number of lags we need to use in equation (17) and (24).

IV. Empirical Results

1. Data

The estimation and hypothesis testing are conducted by a GAUSS program using an IBM PS/2. To cut down computing time, the securities selected into our panel data sets are a subset of stocks contained in the December 1988 version of the CRSP monthly return file. We construct seven panel data sets, with the first three panels A, B & C covering the time periods of 1966.10-1968.12, 1972.10-1974.12 and 1973.10-1975.12, respectively. These time periods are chosen to make our study comparable to that of Reinganum (1981), who found the existence of a "size anomaly" with the APT model. Panels J and J' cover the period of 1985.10-1987.12, while panels K and K' cover the period of 1986.10-1988.12. Panels J' and K' are only used for testing of same factors across groups of securities. We also construct six other panels, D-I, which are used solely for studying the "factor pricing" issue. The time periods covered by the thirteen panels are given in Table 1.

We randomly split the universe of securities listed at the end of each panel time period into four groups. Each security has an equal chance of being selected into any of the four groups. Then, we randomly pick one or two of these groups to construct our panel data set. Securities with missing information on returns, prices and shares outstanding during the time period covered by the panel are excluded. There are about 300 securities in each panel and each panel covers a time period of 27 months. Table 1 provides some further details about the data.

Table 2 presents some summary statistics for some of our panel data. From the top panel of Table 2, we can see that the largest firms in our panels are about 10,000 times as large as the smallest firms. The bottom panel of the table gives the cross-sectional correlation between returns and their lags for 1968.1-1968.12. One can see that 22 out of the total 65 Pearson correlation coefficients are significant at the 5% level. (Significance levels are calculated by treating $(N-2)^{1/2}\rho/(1-\rho^2)^{1/2}$ as coming from a t-distribution with N-2 degrees of freedom, where N is the appropriate sample size and ρ is the Pearson correlation coefficient.) This confirms the theoretical presumption from equation (5) that returns are correlated cross-sectionally with their lags.

2. Estimation of Regression (17) and Test of Minimum Lag Length, K.

Using the data sets constructed above, we estimate (17) for the latest 12 months of each panel (A,B,C,J,K) and use the earlier 15 months data for lags and instruments. Thus (17) is estimated for 1968, 1974, 1975, 1987 and 1988. Although it might be desirable for us to estimate (17) for the 12 months simultaneously, restrictions on matrix size imposed by the GAUSS software prevent us from doing that. So we first do the estimation for the first six months of each year and then for the rest of the year, which means estimating the regression 6 months at a time. Thus there will be 10 sets (2 x 5 years) of regressions (17) in our study, covering a total 10 time periods of 60 month (10 x 6 months). The time periods covered are given in the first column of Table 4.

Table 3 presents the test results of how many lags we should use in the regressions for the two six months periods of 1988. The first column of Table 3a and 3b specifies the number of lag length, K, in the regression. The second column gives the generalized sum of squared residuals, Q, corresponding to each specification. The third column provides the difference in the generalized sum of squared residuals between its corresponding specification and the specification above it, which has one more lag. It measures the reduction in the generalized sum of squared residuals by the introduction of one more lag into the regression. For example, $L_{(K=6,3a)} = Q_{(K=6,3a)} - Q_{(K=7,3a)} = 54.370 - 41.475 = 12.895$. If the specification is true, we expect L to be small. Under the null hypothesis, L has a χ^2 distribution with degrees of freedom given by the fourth column. The last column gives the significance level by which the specification can be rejected.

We start by estimating (17) with K=7. Although it might be desirable to begin with a larger K, the GAUSS software is unable to handle the inverse of the weighting matrix, Ω, (see Appendix for the estimation procedure) whose size increases rapidly with the number of lags and number of months estimated in the regression. As Table 3a and 3b show, we can not reject the hypothesis that equation (17) might have 7 lags for the first six month of 1988 and have 5-7 lags for the rest of the year. For example, the L value for K=6 (11.239) in 3b tells us that we can not reject K=6 at any significance level less than 5%(P=0.081). But the specification of K=4 is strongly rejected(P=0.000), suggesting equation (17) needs at least 5 lags for the period of 1988.7-1988.12. This indicates there are at least 5 systematic factors at work in the market during this time period.

Applying the same procedure to the other 8 time periods, we find the minimum number of lags in the equation seem to change over time, suggesting that the number of factors explaining security returns in the APT model vary over time. The results are provided in the second column of Table 4.

3. Test of Identity of Factors across Two Groups of Securities

Table 5a presents two estimates of equation (17) using data from panels K and K' for the same time period of 1988.7-1988.12. According to our theoretical results in section III, the two estimates should be very close if the APT is true. The estimate for panel K is given by the first line of each row block, while that for panel K' is given by the second line. One can see clearly that some estimated coefficients differ significantly. To be more conclusive, we have performed a joint test of $\psi_{jt}= \omega_{jt}$ for the four time periods estimated and for several specifications of lag length. The test results are given in Table 5b.

The test statistic we use is the Wald test. Denoting the estimated coefficients vector of (17) for panel K(or J) to be H_1, and that for panel K'(or J'), H_2. Denoting their respective variance-covariance matrix to be Θ_1 and Θ_2 and the variance-covariance matrix for $H_1 - H_2$ to be Θ_D. If equation (17) is well specified, then, H_1 and H_2 will be uncorrelated with each other, since the error terms of (17) for panels K (or J) and K'(or J') are uncorrelated. Thus:

$$W= (H_1 - H_2)' \Theta_D^{-1} (H_1 - H_2),$$

where $\Theta_D = \Theta_1 + \Theta_2$.

From Table 5b, we can see that hypothesis $\psi_{jt}= \omega_{jt}$ is strongly rejected for all time periods and for all specification of lag length. Although we can interpret this as a strong evidence against the APT model, we should bear in mind that the above test is a test on the assumptions of the APT. Thus we should not reject the APT as we should not reject the CAPM by simply observing that investors have different believes about the market.

4. Test of "Constancy of Risk Free Rate"

Table 6 presents the results for the test of constant risk free rate with λ_0 known, which is (21), and with λ_0 unknown, which is (23). In Table 6a, we provide the Wald statistics of test (21) on the last six months of 1988. We also provide the Wald statistics for the joint test of (21) being true during the whole period. Since we can not tell precisely how many risk factors there are in the market (or how many lags we should use in equation (17)), we give the results for K=4-7. The constant risk free rate used is 0.005 per month, equivalent to an annual rate of 6%.

From the table, we can see (21) is rejected for three month out of the six month tested for K=4 and two month for K=5. The rejection only happens once for K=6 and 7. Test (21) is also rejected in the joint test for K=4 -7.

The same test is performed on other 9 time periods as well. The second and third column of Table 6c gives the summary results about how many months (and periods) in which (21) is rejected for the 60 months (10 time periods) of study. One can see it is rejected for 28 out of the 60 months tested, for K=4 , and only for 15 month for K=7. The number of rejections is a monotone decreasing function of K. If (21) is true and the test is *independent* over the time periods, (which probably is not true), we expect a rejection of about 3 months (60 x 5%) under 5% significance level, due to sampling errors. Thus, we conclude that (21) is probably rejected for $K \leq 7$. The joint test seems to lean towards a stronger rejection, with (21) being rejected in all 10 periods of our study for K=4 and 9 out of the 10 periods for K=7.

Table 6b provides the Wald statistics for testing hypothesis (23), which is derived from (21) without assuming λ_0 to be observable. The monthly test of (23) rejects the hypothesis three times during the first six month of 1988 for K=4 and once for K=6. The joint test also rejects (23) for K=4 and 6.

Repeating the test for the other 9 time periods, we summarize our findings in the last two column of Table 6c. There, the rejection of (23) is much less frequent than that of (21). The results again suggest the rejection of (23) for K=4 and 5, but they seem to be inconclusive for K=6 and 7.

We don't think the rejection of the"constant risk free rate" is strong evidence against the APT model. It may just reflect the fact that the risk free rate does change over time.

5. A Reexamination of the "Size Anomaly"

The "firm size effect" was documented by Banz (1981), Keim (1983) and Brown, Kleidon and Marsh (1985) in their study of the CAPM. Whether that "size effect" can be captured by the factor loadings of the APT model is still an unsettled problem. In their study of the APT model, Chen (1983) and Chan, Chen and Hsieh (1985)[4] found little size effect after making risk adjustments by factor loadings. But using a same data set and a slightly different approach, Reinganum (1981)

----

[4] Risk factors were assumed to be observable in their studies.

still found large positive excess return in the APT model associated with small firms. In a later work by Lehmann and Modest (1985), they claimed to have found similar results as Reinganum.

As pointed out in our introduction, these previous studies suffer several statistical problems which might lead to the difference in their conclusions concerning the "size anomaly". Here, we will reexamine this issue via the approach we developed in section III, which is to test $\pi_t = 0$ in the regression of (24).

Table 7 presents the test statistics for 1988. Since we can not tell how many risk factors are in the market, we will test $\pi_t = 0$ based on several specifications of K. The second column of Table 7a nad 7b gives the generalized sum of squared residuals, Q, of regression(24). The third column gives the difference in the generalized sum of squared residuals of the restricted ($\pi_t = 0$) model, which is regression (17), and the unrestricted model. The generalized sum of squared residuals of the restricted model, Q, is given in Table 3. Thus, we calculate $L_{(K=4, 7a)} = Q_{(K=4, 3a)} - Q_{(K=4, 7a)} = 88.115 - 68.033 = 20.082$, etc.

From Table 7, we can see that $\pi_t = 0$ is rejected for $K \leq 7$ for the first six months of 1988 and it is also rejected for K=4 and 5, but not for K=6 and 7, for the rest of the year. So our interpretation is that the introduction of more risk factors into the APT model can capture the size effect found in models with less risk factors, though we need $K > 7$ for the first six months of 1988 to capture that effect.

Table 8 presents the estimate of equation (24) for K=4, which confirms our findings in Table 4 that $\pi_t = 0$ is rejected for K=4, for the time period 1988.7-1988.12.

Repeating the test for the other 9 time periods, we summarize our findings in Table 4. One can see clearly that the rejection of $\pi_t = 0$ often happens when the APT model is misspecified, meaning the lag length used in (24) is shorter than the minimum required in regression (17). It is very informative to see that $\pi_t = 0$ is rejected for K=4 for the last six month of 1968, while not rejected for K=5 for the same time period. Since the specification test performed as in Table 3 suggests the requirement of using at least 6 lags in regression (17), it is very possible that the size effect found for (K=4) just picks up those factor loadings omitted from regression (17). Thus, the size anomaly seems to be essentially a misspecification problem, i.e., a failure to properly account for a variety of systematic risks.

It is worth noting here that the first three years (6 time periods) of our study, 1968, 1974, 1975, are those years in which Reinganum found the strongest evidence of size anomaly. While it is possible that our test has little power in rejecting $\pi_t = 0$ for high K, it is also likely Reinganum's size effect may come from his assumption of $K \leq 5$ or is merely a statistical artifact. Thus, our results here are quite supportive to the APT.

6) Test of "Factor Pricing"

To test if the unconditional mean of ψ_{jt} are zero, we estimate (17) for the latest 12 months of each panel (A,B,D,E,F,G,H,I,K) and use the earlier 15 month data for lags and instruments. Thus (17) is estimated for 1968, 1974, 1976, 1978, 1980, 1982, 1984, 1986 and 1988. As before, we first do the estimation for the first six months of each year and then the rest of the year, which means estimating (17) 6 months at a time. Thus there are 18 sets (2 x 9 years) of ψ_{jt} estimates in our study.

We will make estimates from the first six months of the years(9 sets) as our first sample and the others as our second sample. Table 9a gives the time periods from which each sets of ψ_{jt} are estimated. Notice the time periods used in each sample are non-overlapped. This guarantees the estimated ψ_{jt} within each sample will be independent. Each sets of estimates contain 6K number of estimates, with K being the lag length specified in the autoregression.

What we do next is to calculate the sample mean and standard deviation of ψ_{jt} by taking ψ_{jt} from the same month and same j in the sample and calculate the t-statistics. Thus we obtain 6K number of t-statistics from both samples. Under the null hypothesis of all factor premia being zero, the t-statistics should approximately have a t-distribution with 8 degrees of freedom. Table 9b presents the significance level calculated from the first sample for K=4.

From Table 9b, we can see that the test fails to reject E{ ψ_{jt}}=0 for all lagged coefficients of January. But it is rejected for three lagged coefficients of February. Out of the total 24 ψ_{jt} tested for the first sample with K=4, we only find 4 rejections, which is a rejection rate of only 17%.

In Table 9c, we summarize our results from the two samples and present the number of rejections of "E{ ψ_{jt}}=0" for different specification of K and different time of year. As the Table show, we only reject 4 out of total 48 tests for K=4 and 12 out of 84 tests for K=7. Even if our previous study may rule out the case of K=4, the rejection rate for K ≥ 5 is still only slightly higher than the 10% significance level we use. Thus the evidence here in support of the "factor pricing" is quite weak.

We suspect that this test probably does not have much power because of the enormous variation of the ψ_{jt} estimates. The variation comes from two sources: the estimation error from the autoregression and ψ_{jt}'s own random variation. Also the violation of f_t being i.i.d. over time is also going to undermine our tests. Thus, we should interpret the results here with caution.

V. The Robustness of the Methodology to Changes in Beta

Up till now, our study has been based on the assumption that betas are constant over time. However, there are many good reasons to question the validity of this assumption. Changes in a firm's debt-equity ratio, the introduction of new products, mergers and acquisitions, to name a few, all affect firm's sensitivity to changes in pervasive economic forces in the economy. Thus, betas should change over time. How does this affect the results and the applicability of our previous study ?

The answer is probably not much, if the betas follow some well behaved stochastic process. In what follows, we will illustrate this point by using an example of a one factor model. We will extend a same results to the multi-factor model in Appendix II.

Suppose that asset returns are generated by stochastic process (13) with factor loadings varying over time and K=1:

$$R_{it} = \alpha_{i,t} + f_t \beta_{it} + \varepsilon_{it} \qquad\qquad i = 1,...,N; t=1,...,T. \quad (27)$$

The APT imposes a constraint on the parameters of the process:

$$\alpha_{i,t} = \lambda_{0t} + \lambda_{1t} \beta_{it}.$$

Substituting this into (27), we obtain:

$$R_{it} = \lambda_{0t} + (f_t + \lambda_{1t}) \beta_{it} + \varepsilon_{it}. \qquad\qquad i = 1,...,N; t=1,...,T. \quad (28)$$

Assume the evolution of β_{it} follows an AR(1) process with time varying parameters:

$$\beta_{it} = \gamma_t + \phi_t \beta_{it-1} + \xi_{it}. \qquad\qquad i = 1,...,N; t=1,...,T. \quad (29)$$

where $\qquad E(\xi_{it}) = 0, \qquad E(\xi_{is} \xi_{jt}) = \sigma_i^2 \quad$ if i=j and s=t
$$= 0.$$

Although model (29) is restrictive in assuming all firms' risk sensitivity change in the same pattern, it does allow idiosyncratic changes.

If model (29) is well specified, then, we will be able to use information about beta conveyed in historical returns and do the same autoregression analysis as before.

Substituting (29) into (28), and collecting terms, we obtain:

$$R_{it} = \lambda_{0t} + (f_t + \lambda_{1t}) \gamma_t + (f_t + \lambda_{1t}) \phi_t \beta_{it-1} + \varepsilon_{it} + (f_t + \lambda_{1t}) \xi_{it}. \qquad (30)$$

Taking (28) for *time period t-1*, solving for β_{it-1}, we have:

$$\beta_{it-1} = (R_{it-1} - \lambda_{0t-1} - \varepsilon_{i,t-1}) / (f_{t-1} + \lambda_{1t-1}) \qquad (31)$$

Substituting (31) into (30) *for time t*, and denoting:

$$\phi_{0t} = \lambda_{0t} - (f_t + \lambda_{1t}) \phi_t \lambda_{0t-1} / (f_{t-1} + \lambda_{1t-1}) + (f_t + \lambda_{1t}) \gamma_t,$$

$$\phi_{1t} = (f_t + \lambda_{1t}) \phi_t / (f_{t-1} + \lambda_{1t-1}),$$

$$\tau_{it} = \varepsilon_{it} + (f_t + \lambda_{1t}) \xi_{it} - (f_t + \lambda_{1t}) \phi_t \varepsilon_{i,t-1} / (f_{t-1} + \lambda_{1t-1}),$$

we have:

$$R_{it} = \phi_{0t} + \phi_{1t} R_{it-1} + \tau_{it}. \qquad i = 1,...,N; \; t=1,...,T. \qquad (32)$$

It is obvious that ϕ_{0t} and ϕ_{1t} are constant across firms and τ_{it} are uncorrelated across firms and has a mean of zero, conditional on f_t and ϕ_t, since τ_{it} is a linear function of several idiosyncratic shocks.

Comparing (32) with equation (17) for K=1, we can see that they are almost identical except there is one more idiosyncratic term in τ_{it}, $(f_t + \lambda_{1t}) \xi_{it}$, which simply adds some variance to the error term. This is automatically accounted for by our estimation procedure, which allows heteroskedasticity in the error term of (17). It is easy to see that most of our tests are still applicable even if the parameters ϕ_{1t} in (32) are slightly different from that of ψ_{1t} in (17) with K=1. The two exceptions are the "factor pricing test" and the "test of constancy of risk free rate". The first needs an extra assumption of ϕ_t being uncorrelated with f_t, and the second requires γ_t being zero. These requirements may or may not be met in practice. But as a whole, the methodology is still useful even if the betas are time-varying and the results are fairly robust.

VI. Conclusion

In this study, an autoregressive approach is developed to test the APT, allowing for variable-risk-premia. The empirical study find that the minimum number of systematic factors explaining security returns in the APT model varies over time and there are at least 5-7 factors at work in the market during the time periods covered by the study. The APT is found to be capable of capturing the "firm size effect". The test of "factor pricing" only finds weak evidence in support of the APT and is not conclusive. It is also found that the risk free interest rate is time-varying.

These results are derived from a much simpler framework and easier estimation procedure, than those used in previous studies. The paper shows that one can test the central implications of the APT without going through the tedious and problematic procedure of estimating assets' betas. No assumptions are made about the distribution of factors or the constancy of risk premia. The results are proved to be robust to changes in factor loadings in some cases.

Although this new method has many advantages over previous studies, it certainly has its limitations. It does not provide estimates of the betas, which can be interesting for some purposes. The statistical power of this autoregressive method, compared to others, also needs some careful study.

26

References

Brown, Stephen J. and Mark T. Weinstein, 1983, "A New Approach to Testing Arbitrage Pricing Models: The Bilinear Paradigm," Journal of Finance, 38, 711-743.

Brown, P., A. Kleidon and T. Marsh, 1983, "New Evidence on the nature of Size Related Anomalies in Stock Prices", Journal of Financial Economics, 12, 33-56.

Burmeister, Edwin and Marjorie B. McElroy, 1988, "Joint Test of Factor Sensitivities and Risk Premia for the Arbitrage Pricing Theory." Journal of Finance, 43, 721-733.

Campbell, John Y., 1987, "Stock Returns and the Term Structure", Journal of Financial Economics, 18, 373-399.

Chamberlain, Gary, 1983, "Panel Data," Chapter 22 in the handbook of Econometrics Volume II, ed. by Z. Griliches and M. Intrilligator. Amsterdam: North-Holland Publishing Company.

Chan, K.C., Nai-fu Chen and David Hsieh, 1985, "An Exploratory Investigation of the Firm Size Effect" Journal of Financial Economics, 14, 451-471.

Chen, Nai-fu, 1983, "Some Empirical Tests of the Theory of Arbitrage Pricing." Journal of Finance, 38, 1392-1414.

Chen, Nai-fu, Richard Roll and Stephen Ross, 1986, "Economic Forces and the Stock Market ." Journal of Business, 59, 386-403.

Cho, Chinhyung D. and William Taylor, 1987,"The Seasonal Stability of the Factor Structure of Stock Returns", Journal of Finance, 42, 1195-1211.

Cho, Chinhyung D., Edwin J. Elton and Martin J. Gruber, 1984,"On the Robustness of the Roll and Ross Arbitrage Pricing Theory", Journal of Financial and Quantitative Analysis, 19, 1-10.

Connor, Gregory and Robert A. Korajczyk, 1988, "Risk and Return in an Equilibrium APT: Application of a New Test Methodology" Journal of Financial Economics, 21, 255-289.

Cragg, John and Burton Malkiel, 1982, "Expectations and the Structure of Share Prices." University of Chicago Press.

Dhrymes, Pheobus F., Irwin Friend and N. Bulent Gultekin, 1984," A Critical Reexamination of the Empirical Evidence on the Arbitrage Pricing Theory", Journal of Finance, 39, 323-346.

Fama, E.and J. MacBeth, 1973,"Risk, Return and Equilibrium: Empirical Tests", Journal of Political Economy, 81, 607-636.

Gibbons, Michael R.,1982, "Multivariate Test of Financial Models: A New Approach", Journal of Financial Economics, 10, 3-27.

Gibbons, Michael R. and Wayne Ferson, 1985, "Testing Asset Pricing Models with Changing Expectations and an Unobservable Market Portfolio", Journal of Financial Economics, 14, 217-236.

Gultekin, Mustafa N. and N. Bulent Gultekin, 1987,"Stock Return Anomalies and Tests of the APT", Journal of Finance, 42, 1213-1224.

Huberman, Gur, 1982,"Arbitrage Pricing Theory: A Simple Approach." Journal of Economic Theory, 28, 183-191.

Huberman, Gur, Shmuel Kandel and Robert Stambaugh, 1987, "Mimicking Portfolios and Exact Arbitrage Pricing", Journal of Finance, 42, 1-9.

Holtz-Eakin, Douglas , Whitney Newey and Harvey Rosen, 1988 ,"Estimating Vector Autoregressions with Panel Data", Econometrica, 56,1371-1395.

Keim, Donald B., 1983, "Size Related Anomalies and Stock Return Seasonality: Empirical Evidence", Journal of Financial Economics, 12, 13-32.

Lehmann, Bruce N. and David M. Modest, 1985, "The Empirical Foundations of the Arbitrage Pricing Theory I: The Empirical Tests". NBER Working Paper No. 1725.

Jobson, J.O., 1982, "A Multivariate Linear Regression Test for the Arbitrage Pricing Theory", Journal of Finance, 37, 1037-1042.

McElroy Marjorie B. and Edwin Burmeister, 1988, "Arbitrage Pricing Theory as a Restricted Nonlinear Multivariate Regression Model: ITNLSUR Estimates", Journal of Business and Economic Statistics, 6, 29-42

Mei, Jianping, 1989, "Variable-Expected Returns and the Present Value Model: A Panel Study, " Financial Research Center Working Paper #107, Princeton University.

Miller, Merton H. and Myron Scholes, 1972, "Rates of Return in Relation to Risk: A Re-examination of Some Recent Findings." in Michael C. Jensen, ed. Studies in the Theory of Capital Markets.. New YorK: Praeger.

Reinganum, Mark, 1981, "The Arbitrage Pricing Theory: Some Empirical Results", Journal of Finance, 36, 313-321.

Roll, Richard, 1977,"A Criteque of the Asset Pricing's Tests", Journal of Financial Economics, 4, 120-176.

Roll, Richard and Stephen A. Ross, 1980, "An Empirical Investigation of the Arbitrage Pricing Theory", Journal of Finance, 35, 1073-1103.

Ross, Stephen, 1976, "The Arbitrage Theory of Capital Asset Pricing", Journal of Economic Theory, 13, 341-360.

Shanken, Jay, 1985, "Multivariate Tests of The Zero-Beta CAPM", Journal of Financial Economics, 14, 327-348.

White, Halbert ,1980,"A Heteroskedasticity-consistent Covariance Matrix Estimator and a Direct Test for Heterokedasticity", Econometrica, 48, 817-838.

Appendix I

Here, we will present the estimation procedure developed by H, N & R, under which autoregression (24) can be estimated and restrictions tested. Using their notation, we write:

$$Y_t = (R_{1,t}, R_{2,t}, \dots R_{N,t})' \qquad\qquad X_t = (C_{1,t}, C_{2,t}, \dots, C_{N,t})'$$

as Nx1 vectors of observations for a given time period t .

Let $W_t = (e, Y_{t-1}, \dots, Y_{t-K}, X_{t-1})$. They are the RHS variables of (24). e is a Nx1 vector of ones.

Let $U_t = (\eta_{1,t}, \eta_{2,t}, \dots, \eta_{N,t})'$ be the transformed error terms, and let $B_t = (\psi_{0t}, \psi_{1t}, \dots \psi_{Kt}, \pi_t)'$. Then equation (24) can be written as:

$$Y_t = W_t B_t + U_t . \qquad\qquad t = K+1, \dots, T . \qquad\qquad (A1)$$

To combine equation (A1) over time into system of equations, we "stack" equation (A1) by time and denote:

$$Y = (Y_{K+1}', \dots, Y_T')' ; \qquad\qquad ((T-K)Nx1)$$

$$B = (B_{K+1}', \dots, B_T')' ; \qquad\qquad ((T-K)(K+1)x1)$$

$$U = (U_{K+1}', \dots, U_T')' ; \qquad\qquad ((T-K)Nx1)$$

$$W = diag (W_{K+1}', \dots, W_T') ; \qquad\qquad ((T-K)Nx(T-K)(K+1))$$

where diag $(W_{K+1}', \dots, W_T')$ denotes a block diagonal matrix with $W_{K+1}', \dots, W_T'$ placed on the diagonal. Thus equation (24) can be written as :

$$Y = WB + U . \qquad\qquad\qquad (A2)$$

To estimate (A2), H, N & R proposed a linear 3SLS procedure which is quite similar to the conventional 3SLS procedure for estimating simultaneous equations. In the first two stage, a generalized instrumental variable estimation procedure is used to obtain a consistent estimate of B_t of equation (A1) for all time periods:

$$\tilde{B}_t = [W_t{'}Z_t(Z_t{'}Z_t)^{-1}Z_t{'}W_t]^{-1}W_t{'}Z_t(Z_t{'}Z_t)^{-1}Z_t{'}Y_t . \quad t=K+1,...,T. \qquad \text{(A3)}$$

where Z_t is a matrix composed of variables in $\{\Theta, Y_{t-K-1},..., Y_1, X_{t-K-1},..., X_1\}$ as its column vectors.

At the third stage, the residuals from the above regression for (A3), $V_t = Y_t - W_t\tilde{B}_t$, is used to calculate a White–type weighting matrix for equations (A2):

$$\tilde{\Omega} = \sum_{j=1}^{N} \tilde{v}_{jr}\tilde{v}_{js}Z_{jr}{'}Z_{js},\qquad \text{(A4)}$$

where Z_{jt} $(t=s,r)$ is the jth row of Z_t and $\tilde{v}_{jt}$ is the jth element of $\tilde{V}_t$. Then, the generalized instrumental variable estimation procedure is used again to get a consistent and more efficient estimate of B in equations (A3):

$$\hat{B} = [W'Z(\tilde{\Omega})^{-1}Z'W]^{-1}W'Z(\tilde{\Omega})^{-1}Z'Y \qquad \text{(A5)}$$

Its asymptotic variance and covariance matrix is given by:

$$\Theta = \text{Var}(\hat{B}) = [W'Z(\tilde{\Omega})^{-1}Z'W]^{-1} \qquad \text{(A6)}$$

Equation (17) can be estimated with essentially the same procedure.

The test of how many lags should be in equation (24) and whether $\pi_t = 0$ can be treated as testing zero constraints on the coefficients of (24). For these problems, our test strategy is pretty similar to that of the Chow-type test. We first estimate the unrestricted and the restricted model and then calculate and compare the difference in the sum of squared residuals. We denote:

$$Q = (Y-W\hat{B})'Z(\tilde{\Omega})^{-1}Z'(Y-W\hat{B}) / N \qquad \text{(A7)}$$

which is the generalized sum of squared residuals of system (A2). We calculate L $= Q_R - Q_U$, where Q_R and Q_U are respectively the generalized sum of squard residuals of the restricted and unrestricted systems. If the restricted model is true, we expect L to be small. Under the null hypothesis, L follows a χ^2 distribution with degrees of freedom equal to the difference between the number of coefficients to be estimated in the two systems. Thus, we use the following testing procedure: If $L > L_\alpha$, we reject H_0. See H, N & R's paper for details.

Appendix II

Assume that capital markets are perfectly competitive and frictionless. Asset returns are generated by the linear factor model (13) with time-varying betas:

$$R_{it} = \alpha_{i,t} + f_{1t}\beta_{i1t} + \ldots + f_{Kt}\beta_{iKt} + \varepsilon_{it} \qquad i = 1,\ldots,N; \ t = 1,\ldots,T. \qquad (B1)$$

The APT imposes a linear constraint on the parameters of the model:

$$\alpha_{i,t} = \lambda_{0t} + \lambda_{1t}\beta_{i1t} + \ldots + \lambda_{Kt}\beta_{iKt}. \qquad (B2)$$

Substituting (B2) into (B1) and denote $s_t' = (s_{1t},\ldots,s_{Kt}) = (f_{1t},\ldots,f_{Kt}) + (\lambda_{1t},\ldots,\lambda_{Kt})$ and $\beta_{it}' = (\beta_{i1t},\ldots,\beta_{iKt})$, we obtain,

$$R_{i,t} = \lambda_{0t} + s_t'\beta_{it} + \varepsilon_{i,t}. \qquad i=1,\ldots,N; \ t=1,\ldots,T. \qquad (B3)$$

Assume the evolution of β_{it} follows a multi-variate AR(1) process with time-varying parameters:

$$\beta_{it} = \gamma_t + \phi_t\beta_{it-1} + \xi_{it}. \qquad i = 1,\ldots,N; \ t=1,\ldots,T.$$

where γ_t and ϕ_t are Kx1 and KxK matrices, respectively. $E(\xi_{it}) = 0$, $E(\xi_{is}\xi_{jt}') = \Gamma_i$ for i=j and s=t, otherwise, $E(\xi_{is}\xi_{jt}') = 0$. Γ_i is a KxK matrix.

To replace β_{it} in (B1) with "proxies" constructed from the historical return information, we notice that:

$$\beta_{it} = \phi_t\phi_{t-1}\cdots\phi_{t-q+1}\beta_{i,t-q} + \gamma_t + \sum_{J=1}^{q-1}\phi_t\cdots\phi_{t-J+1}\gamma_{t-J} + \xi_{it} + \sum_{J=1}^{q-1}\phi_t\cdots\phi_{t-J+1}\xi_{i,t-J}. \quad q\geq 2. \quad (B4)$$

As in Section III, we take equation (B3) from t-1 and t-K, and replace all β_{it} by β_{it-k} using (B4), we obtain:

$$R_{i,t-1} = \lambda'_{0,t-1} + s_{t-1}'\phi_{t-1}\cdots\phi_{t-k+2}\beta_{i,t-K} + \mu_{i,t-1}$$
$$\vdots \qquad \vdots$$
$$R_{i,t-K} = \lambda'_{0,t-K} + s_{t-K}'\beta_{i,t-K} + \mu_{i,t-K}$$

where μ_{is} is just a linear function of ε_{is}, s_s, current and past ϕ_q, $\xi_{iq}(t-K \leq q \leq s)$

and λ'_{0s} is just a linear function of λ_{0s} and s_s, current and past ϕ_q, $\gamma_q (t-K \leq q \leq s)$.

$$\text{Denoting} \quad S_t = \begin{bmatrix} s'_{t-1}\phi_{t-1} \cdots \phi_{t-K+1} \\ \vdots \\ s'_{t-k} \end{bmatrix} \qquad \Pi_t = \begin{bmatrix} R_{i,t-1} - \lambda'_{qt-1} - \mu_{i,t-1} \\ \vdots \\ R_{i,t-K} - \lambda'_{qt-K} - \mu_{i,t-K} \end{bmatrix}$$

S_t is a KxK matrix and Π_{it} is a Kx1 matrix. Thus, we have,

$$S_t \beta_{i,t-K} = \Pi_{it}.$$

Assume S_t is non- singular. We solve for $\beta_{i,t-K}$,

$$\beta_{i,t-K} = S_t^{-1} \Pi_{it}. \tag{B5}$$

Since $R_{i,t} = \lambda'_{0t} + s'_t \phi_t \cdots \phi_{t-K+1}\beta_{it-K} + \mu_{i,t}$, we substitute (B5) into it and obtain:

$$R_{i,t} = \lambda'_{0t} + s'_t \phi_t \cdots \phi_{t-K+1}S_t^{-1} \Pi_{it} + \mu_{i,t}. \quad i=1,\dots, N, \ t=K+1,\dots,T.$$

Collecting terms, and define $\varphi_t' =(\varphi_{1t} ,\dots, \varphi_{Kt})= s'_t \phi_t \cdots \phi_{t-K+1}S_t^{-1}$, we have:

$$R_{i,t} = \varphi_{0t} + \sum_{j=1}^{K} \varphi_{jt} R_{i,t-j} + \tau_{i,t}. \quad i=1,\dots,N; \quad t=K+1,\dots,T. \tag{B6}$$

Where: $\quad \varphi_{0,t} = \lambda'_{0t} - \sum_{j=1}^{K} \varphi_{jt} \lambda'_{0,t-j} \qquad \tau_{i,t} = \mu_{it} - \sum_{j=1}^{K} \varphi_{jt} \mu_{i,t-j}. \qquad t=K+1,\dots,T.$

It is obvious that $\varphi_{0,t}$ and φ_{jt} are constant across firms and $\tau_{i,t}$ are uncorrelated across firms and has a mean of zero, since $\tau_{i,t}$ is a linear function of several idiosyncratic shocks.

Comparing (B6) with equation (17), we can see that they are almost identical except that the error term is much noisier. This will not affect our estimation procedure, which allows heteroskedasticity in the error term. It is easy to show that most of our tests are still applicable even if the parameters φ_{jt} in (B6) are slightly different from that of ψ_{jt} in (17). The two exceptions are the "factor pricing test" and the "test of constancy of risk free rate". The first needs an extra assumption of ϕ_t being uncorrelated with f_t, while the second requires all γ_t being zero.

Table 1. Description of Data

==

Source: Center for Research in Security Prices
        Graduate School of Business
        University of Chicago
        Monthly Return File

Selection Criteria: By random selection. Firms selected must have complete
                information on returns and capitalization for the entire
                panel time span.

Variables selected	a) Return(including dividends) of the month $R_{i,t}$
from the file:	b) Month end closing price, $P_{i,t}$
	c) Shares outstanding, $N_{i,t}$

Variables constructed: a) log capitalization, $\zeta_{i,t} = \log(P_{i,t} N_{i,t})$.

Number of securities included and time periods covered by the panels:

Panel	A	B	C	D	E
Securities	293	267	286	364	352
Time span	66.10-68.12	72.10-74.12	73.10-75.12	74.10-76.12	76.10-78.12

F	G	H	I	J	K
359	348	355	324	308	298
78.10-80.12	80.10-82.12	82.10-84.12	84.10-86.12	85.10-87.12	86.10-88.12

Control panels J' and K' cover the same time period as J and K but include 318
             and 304 securities, respectively.

==

Table 2. Summary Statistics for the Panel Data Set

a). The Capitalization of the Smallest and Largest Firms in Our Panels(million)

Panel	A	B	C	J	K
Min.	11.742	3.001	3.274	2.519	3.165
Max.	22612.2	24965.4	28832.1	29978.8	36303.1

b). Cross-sectional Correlation of Returns(based on returns from 68.1-68.12)

Ret.	R1	R2	R3	R4	R5	R6	R7	R8	R9	R10	R11	R12
R1	*	0.05	0.00	0.02	0.06	0.02	0.00	0.01	0.85	0.59	0.34	0.00
R2	-0.11	*	0.71	0.00	0.01	0.97	0.00	0.90	0.37	0.59	0.00	0.00
R3	-0.18	-0.02	*	0.79	0.43	0.54	0.11	0.16	0.43	0.81	0.08	0.09
R4	-0.13	-0.20	-0.02	*	0.81	0.00	0.00	0.00	0.34	0.67	0.27	0.00
R5	0.11	-0.16	-0.05	0.01	*	0.33	0.00	0.24	0.50	0.42	0.64	0.15
R6	0.13	0.00	-0.04	-0.21	-0.06	*	0.00	0.14	0.16	0.66	0.00	0.04
R7	0.30	0.18	-0.09	-0.18	-0.16	0.21	*	0.53	0.55	0.93	0.69	0.87
R8	0.15	0.00	-0.08	0.18	0.07	-0.08	0.04	*	0.72	0.27	0.07	0.02
R9	0.01	-0.05	0.05	0.05	-0.04	-0.08	0.03	-0.02	*	0.18	0.86	0.52
R10	0.03	-0.03	-0.01	-0.02	0.05	-0.03	0.00	0.06	-0.08	*	0.89	0.82
R11	-0.06	-0.17	-0.10	-0.07	-0.03	0.18	0.02	-0.11	-0.01	0.00	*	0.00
R12	0.16	0.15	-0.10	-0.16	0.08	-0.12	0.00	-0.14	0.04	-0.01	-0.21	*

Note: R1-R12 represents returns from 68.1-68.12. The lower part of the diagonal gives the cross-sectional correlation of returns, while the upper part gives the significance level by which the corresponding correlations are different from zero.

Table 3. Test of Lag Length K in equation (17)

$$R_{i,t} = \psi_{0t} + \sum_{j=1}^{K} \psi_{jt}\, R_{i,t-j} + \eta_{i,t}\,. \qquad i=1,...,N; \quad t=K+1,...,T. \qquad (17)$$

a). 1988.1-1988.6

Total lags K	Q	L	DF	P
(1) K=7	41.475	_	36	0.244
(2) K=6	54.370	12.895	6	0.044
(3) K=5	85.870	31.437	6	0.000
(4) K=4	88.115	2.308	6	0.889

b). 1988.7-1988.12

Total lags K	Q	L	DF	P
(1) K=7	38.702	_	36	0.348
(2) K=6	49.941	11.239	6	0.081
(3) K=5	62.338	12.397	6	0.054
(4) K=4	154.002	91.664	6	0.000

Note: Returns from lag 8 to lag 15 and log capitalization from lag 8 to lag 12 have been used as instruments. P gives the corresponding χ^2-square probability under which level the H_0 can be rejected.

Table 4. Summary of Tests of Lag Length K in (17) and "Test of Size Effect" for Different Estimation Periods.

$$R_{i,t} = \psi_{0t} + \sum_{j=1}^{K} \psi_{jt} R_{i,t-j} + \eta_{i,t} \, . \qquad i=1,...,N; \quad t=K+1,...,T. \qquad (17)$$

$$R_{i,t} = \psi_{0t} + \sum_{j=1}^{K} \psi_{jt} R_{i,t-j} + \pi_t C_{i,t} + \eta_{i,t} \, . \qquad i=1,...,N; \quad t=K+1,...,T, \qquad (24)$$

Time period	Min. K	K=7($\pi_t = 0$)	K=6 ($\pi_t = 0$)	K=5 ($\pi_t = 0$)	K=4 ($\pi_t = 0$)
68.1-69.6	7	-	R*	R*	R*
68.7-68.12	6	-	-	-	R*
74.1-74.6	6	R	R	R*	R*
74.7-74.12	7	-	R*	R*	R*
75.1-75.6	6	-	-	-	-
75.7-75.12	7	-	R*	R*	R*
87.1-87.6	7	-	-	R*	R*
87.7-87.12	5	-	-	-	-
88.1-88.6	7	R	R*	R*	R*
88.7-88.12	5	-	-	R	R*

Note: Returns from lag 8 to lag 15 and log capitalization from lag 8 to lag 12 have been used as instruments. "R" indicates rejection of hypothesis $\pi_t = 0$ for the time period. Asterisk (*) here indicates the rejection of $\pi_t = 0$ when model (24) is actually misspecified, meaning K < Min. K.

Table 5. Results for the "Same Factors Test" (H_0: $\psi_{jt} = \omega_{jt}$.)
Based on Panels J vs J' and Panels K vs K'

$$R_{i,t} = \psi_{0t} + \sum_{j=1}^{K} \psi_{jt} R_{i,t-j} + \eta_{i,t} \, . \qquad i=1,...,N; \quad t=K+1,...,T.$$

$$(19)$$

$$R_{i,t} = \omega_{0t} + \sum_{j=1}^{K} \omega_{jt} R_{i,t-j} + \eta_{i,t} \, . \qquad i=1,...,N; \quad t=K+1,...,T.$$

a). Estimates of Equation(17) for Panels K and K'(K=4)(1988.7-1988.12)

Dep.var.	cons.	$R_{i,t-1}$	$R_{i,t-2}$	$R_{i,t-3}$	$R_{i,t-4}$
Jan. 1988	0.014	-0.330*	-0.017	-0.332	0.129
$R_{i,t}$	0.026	-0.672*	-0.322	0.427	-0.297
Feb. 1988	-0.014*	-0.712**	-0.138	-0.094	-0.524*
$R_{i,t}$	-0.016	-0.063	-0.304	0.338	-0.433
March 1988	0.012	-0.469	-0.060	0.270	0.102
$R_{i,t}$	0.070**	0.587*	-0.539	-0.665**	-0.050
April 1988	0.003	0.334*	-0.090	0.331*	-0.176
$R_{i,t}$	0.012	-0.117	0.014	0.188	0.035
May 1988	-0.081**	0.197	0.986**	-0.836**	0.228
$R_{i,t}$	-0.039**	0.702**	0.284*	0.050	0.252
June 1988	-0.063**	-1.038**	-0.496	0.823**	-1.486**
$R_{i,t}$	0.006	0.217	0.440	0.385	-0.405

Note: Returns from lag 8 to lag 15 and log capitalization from lag 8 to lag 12 have been used as instruments. We report the estimates of equation (17) for panel K in the first line of each block, and those of panel K' in the second line of each block. We also report those t-values which exceed 2 by indicating them with one asterisk(*) and which exceed 3 by two asterisks(**).

Table 5. Results for the "Same Factors Test" (H_0: $\psi_{jt} = \omega_{jt}$.)
Based on Panels J vs J' and Panels K vs K'(continued)

$$R_{i,t} = \psi_{0t} + \sum_{j=1}^{K} \psi_{jt} R_{i,t-j} + \eta_{i,t} \ . \qquad i=1,...,N; \quad t=K+1,...,T.$$

$$\tag{19}$$

$$R_{i,t} = \omega_{0t} + \sum_{j=1}^{K} \omega_{jt} R_{i,t-j} + \eta_{i,t} \ . \qquad i=1,...,N; \quad t=K+1,...,T.$$

b). Significance levels at which H_0: $\psi_{jt} = \omega_{jt}$ is rejected
for the four time periods.

Time Period	K=4	K=5	K=6	K=7
87.1-87.6	0.000	0.000	0.000	0.000
87.7-87.12	0.000	0.000	0.000	0.000
88.1-88.6	0.000	0.000	0.000	0.000
88.7-88.12	0.000	0.000	0.000	0.000

Note: Returns from lag 8 to lag 15 and log capitalization from lag 8 to lag 12 have been used as instruments. The degrees of freedom (DF) for K=4 is 30, for K=5 is 36, for K=6 is 42 and for K=7 is 48.

Table 6. Results for the "Constant Risk Free Rate Test"

$$\frac{\psi_{0t}}{\lambda_0} + \sum_{j=1}^{K} \psi_{jt} = 1. \qquad t = K+1, \cdots, T. \qquad (21)$$

$$\frac{\psi_{0,t}}{\psi_{0,K+1}}\left(1 - \sum_{j=1}^{K} \psi_{j,K+1}\right) + \sum_{j=1}^{K} \psi_{j,t} = 1. \qquad t = K+2, \cdots, T. \qquad (23)$$

a). Test statistics of (21) for July- Dec. 1988

Factors	July	Aug.	Sept.	Oct.	Nov.	Dec.	Joint Test
K=4	0.961	37.502*	0.244	0.003	48.189*	17.345*	109.718*
K=5	0.606	49.524*	0.097	1.039	0.045	6.089*	69.477*
K=6	1.088	34.518*	0.073	1.653	0.078	1.271	54.145*
K=7	0.003	14.124*	0.834	1.687	0.005	1.952	28.740*

Note: The risk free rate λ_0 used here is 6% per annum. The degrees of freedom for individual month are 1 and that for the joint test is 6. The critical value for individual month is 3.84, for that for the joint test is 12.59, respectively, at 5% significance level. Asterisk(*) indicates the rejection of (21).

b). Test statistics of (23) for July- Dec. 1988

Factors	July	Aug.	Sept.	Oct.	Nov.	Dec.	Joint Test
K=4	-	14.500*	0.015	0.033	4.524*	8.234*	27.871*
K=5	-	0.844	0.030	0.368	0.110	0.525	1.804
K=6	-	22.569*	0.154	1.069	0.015	1.523	30.458*
K=7	-	1.446	0.550	0.596	0.004	0.757	1.634

Note: The degrees of freedom for individual month are 1 and that for the joint test is 5. The cretical value for individual month is 3.84, for that for the joint test is 11.07, respectively, at 5% significance level. Asterisk(*) indicates the rejection of (23).

Table 6. Results for the "Constant Risk Free Rate Test"(continued)

$$\frac{\psi_{0t}}{\lambda_0} + \sum_{j=1}^{K} \psi_{jt} = 1. \qquad t= K+1,\cdots,T. \qquad (21)$$

$$\frac{\psi_{0,t}}{\psi_{0,K+1}}\left(1-\sum_{j=1}^{K} \psi_{j,K+1}\right) + \sum_{j=1}^{K} \psi_{j,t} = 1. \qquad t=K+2,\cdots,T. \qquad (23)$$

c). Number of months(or periods of 6 month) in which
(21) and (23) are Rejected.

Factors	Test of (21) *	Joint Test of (21) *	Test of (23) *	Joint Test of (23)
K=4	28	10	17	6
K=5	23	10	12	5
K=6	19	9	6	5
K=7	15	9	5	4

Note: Number of months tested for (21) is 60, and that for (23) is 50. Number of periods joint tests performed is 10.

Table 7. Results for the "Size Effect Test" ($\pi_t=0$ in equation (24))

$$R_{i,t} = \psi_{0t} + \sum_{j=1}^{K} \psi_{jt} R_{i,t-j} + \pi_t C_{i,t} + \eta_{i,t} \, . \qquad i=1,\dots,N; \quad t=K+1,\dots,T, \qquad (24)$$

a). 1988.1-1988.6

Total lags K	Q	L ($\pi_t=0$)	DF	P
(1) K=4	68.033	20.082	6	0.002
(2) K=5	53.264	32.543	6	0.000
(3) K=6	37.095	17.275	6	0.008
(4) K=7	25.513	15.963	6	0.013

b). 1988.7-1988.12

Total lags K	Q	L ($\pi_t=0$)	DF	P
(1) K=4	120.242	33.760	6	0.000
(2) K=5	45.068	17.270	6	0.001
(3) K=6	40.180	9.761	6	0.135
(4) K=7	32.848	5.854	6	0.439

Note: Returns from lag 8 to lag 15 and log capitalization from lag 8 to lag 12 have been used as instruments. P gives the corresponding χ^2-square probability under which level "$\pi_t=0$" can be rejected.

Table 8. Estimates of Equation (24) for July 88-Dec. 88 (K=4)

$$R_{i,t} = \psi_{0t} + \sum_{j=1}^{K} \psi_{jt} R_{i,t-j} + \pi_t C_{i,t} + \eta_{i,t} \,. \qquad i=1,\dots,N; \quad t=K+1,\dots,T, \qquad (24)$$

Dep.Var.	Cons.	$R_{i,t-1}$	$R_{i,t-2}$	$R_{i,t-3}$	$R_{i,t-4}$	$C_{i,t}$
July 88	-0.086	-0.225	-0.012	-0.563*	0.413**	0.007*
	(-1.801)	(-1.683)	(-0.058)	(-2.979)	(3.277)	(2.223)
Aug. 88	-0.025	-0.673**	-0.069	-0.054	-0.312	0.001
	(-0.758)	(-5.223)	(-0.780)	(-0.360)	(-1.460)	(0.227)
Sept. 88	-0.091	-0.100	-0.245	0.305	-0.316	0.008*
	(-1.807)	(-0.288)	(-0.966)	(1.304)	(-1.111)	(2.411)
Oct. 88	-0.063	0.153	0.312	0.421*	-0.042	0.005*
	(-1.855)	(1.013)	(1.322)	(2.867)	(-0.307)	(2.219)
Nov. 88	-0.231**	-0.516	0.766**	-0.099	0.381	0.012*
	(-3.959)	(-1.507)	(3.824)	(-0.317)	(1.760)	(2.750)
Dec. 88	-0.230*	-1.163**	-1.362**	0.667*	-0.520	0.014*
	(-2.565)	(-4.132)	(-3.229)	(2.521)	(-1.117)	(2.176)

Note: Returns from lag 8 to lag 15 and log capitalization from lag 8 to lag 12 have been used as instruments. T-statistics are given in parentheses. We also report those t-values which exceed 2 by indicating them with one asterisk(*) and those exceed 3 by two asterisks(**).

Table 9. Test of "Factor Pricing"

a). Time Periods from Which Data Are Used to estimate ψ_{jt}

First Sample	set A	set B	set D	set E	set F	set G
Time period	66.10-68.6	72.10-74.6	74.10-76.6	76.10-78.6	78.10-80.6	80.10-82.6

set H	set I	set K	I Second Sample	set A'	set B'	set D'
82.10-84.6	84.10-86.6	86.10-88.6	I Time period	67.4-68.12	73.4-74.12	75.4-76.12

set E'	set F'	set G'	set H'	set I'	set K'
77.4-78.12	79.4-80.12	81.4-82.12	83.4-84.12	85.4-86.12	87.4-88.12

b) P-values for H_0: $E\{\psi_{jt}\}=0$ Calculated from the First Sample (K=4)

Lagged Coef.	ψ_{1t}	ψ_{2t}	ψ_{3t}	ψ_{4t}
Jan.	0.379	0.542	0.832	0.952
Feb.	0.005*	0.635	0.027*	0.099*
March	0.408	0.686	0.353	0.044*
April	0.542	0.151	0.898	0.337
May	0.181	0.479	0.409	0.450
June	0.387	0.943	0.555	0.495

Note: P-values are calculated from a t-statistics which takes the sample mean of estimated ψ_{jt} over nine time periods and divided it by its sample standard error. The t-statistics is assumed to have a t-distribution with 8 degrees of freedom. Asterisk(*) indicates the rejection of H_0: $E\{\psi_{jt}\}=0$ at 10% significance level.

43

Table 9. Test of "Factor Pricing"(continued)

c). Number of Rejections of H_0: E{ ψ_{jt} }=0 for Different Specification of Lag Length and Different time of Year.

Lagged Coef.	K=4	K=5	K=6	K=7
Jan.	0	0	1	0
Feb.	3	2	2	3
March	1	1	0	0
April	0	1	0	0
May	0	0	0	0
June	0	0	1	1
July	0	0	1	2
Aug.	0	0	1	1
Sept.	0	1	1	2
Oct.	0	0	1	0
Nov.	0	1	1	2
Dec.	0	1	1	1
Rejection Rate	4/48=8.3%	7/60=11.6%	10/72=13.9%	12/84=14.2%

Note: The significance level used here is 10%.

Variable-Expected-Returns and the Present Value Model: A Panel Study*

* I would like to thank Gordon Bodnar, Gregory Chow, Dexter Chu, Bill Gentry, Albert Margolis, Whitney Newey and Harvey Rosen for helpful comments. Douglas Holtz-Eakin graciously provided me with the program for panel regression. This research is supported by the John M. Olin Foundation for Study of Economic Organization and Public Policy.

I. Introduction

The empirical investigation of the present value model (PVM) has been going on for almost a decade now, since the publication of the original work by LeRoy and Porter (1981) and Shiller (1981). Up till now, all research has focused on a very special case: "Do price *indexes* behave like an optimal forecast of their underlying dividends if the expected rate of return is *constant* ?" Typically, people find future returns are somewhat predictable and price indexes are too volatile to be justified by changes in future dividends, if the constant-expected-return model is true. (see Mankiw, Romer and Shapiro (1985), Campbell and Shiller (1986), Keim and Stambaugh (1986),West (1987)). But the constant-expected-return model is too simple to be true and the excess volatility of stock price indexes may be due to the movements of expected return.

Trying to take into account the movements of expected return, Campbell and Shiller (1988b) used a linearized version of the PVM and tested three different models of expected return under the assumption that expected return are *observable* ex post: the return on short debt plus a constant, the consumption-based asset-pricing model with constant relative risk aversion, and the return on short debt plus a term that depends on the conditional variance of return. West (1988) also tried the consumption-based asset-pricing model with constant relative risk aversion. Both of them rejected the PVM.

Although the evidence presented against the PVM by their time series studies is quite convincing, we still feel these models are not general enough to make the mission of saving the PVM impossible. We also notice that in the literature very little work has been done to test the model using papel data set, although the PVM not only regulates the *time* evolution of share prices, but also the price *structure* across firms. One major difficulty of pursuing that direction is the obvious problem that expected-returns are *unobservable*. Since they seem to vary greatly from firm to firm and from time to time, we simply can not assume them to be a same function of some observable time series in a panel study.

By taking advantage of recent econometric work by Holtz-Eakin, Newey and Rosen (H, N & R), this paper extends the test of the PVM from time series study to panel study. We will study a more general model of expected returns and its implications on the dividend ratio model, which is a linearized version of the PVM derived by Campbell and Shiller (1988b) (C&S).

The potential payoffs from a panel study seem large. In particular, by taking advantage of panel data, we can employ a more general model of expected returns that allows for both time-varying expected returns and cross-security differences in risk exposures.

With a large body of panel data, we can also drop the crucial assumption in Campbell and Shiller's work that the economy evolves through time as a bivariate process with *constant* coefficients. Instead we allow the coefficients to vary over time. Since many changes in the market can be described as a change in the coefficients of the vector autoregressive (VAR) process, our model can easily incorporate many kinds of regime changes, while the constant coefficients model seems to be too restrictive in coping with the ever-changing economic world.

By incorporating the number of VAR lags into hypothesis testing, we also pay more attention to the specification of lag length. With a large panel data set and the relatively small number of parameters in the model, we should feel more comfortable applying asymptotic distribution theory. Our work is also less vulnerable to the unit-root and explosive root problem often encountered in time series study.

The work will be organized as follows: Part II will specify the dividend ratio model. Part III will provide a framework under which test of model of expected returns can be performed on a panel data set. Part IV will specify the vector autoregressive process and derive constraints imposed on it by the dividend ratio model. Part V will explain the data used and present empirical results. Part VI concludes.

II. The Dividend-Ratio Model

We start by restating C & S' dividend-ratio model. Following their notation, we write the real price of a stock i at the beginning of time period t, as $P_{i,t}$; and the real dividend paid on the stock during the period t, as $D_{i,t}$. Denote the realized log return for holding the stock from beginning of t to the beginning of t+1, as $h_{i,t}$

$$h_{i,t} = \log(P_{i,t+1} + D_{i,t}) - \log(P_{i,t}) . \tag{1}$$

To derive a linearized version of the PVM, we would like to obtain a linear relationship between the realized log return, the log dividend price-ratio and the dividend growth rate. Define $\delta_{i,t} = \log(D_{i,t-1}) - \log(P_{i,t})$, as the dividend-price ratio and $\Delta d_{i,t} = \log(D_{i,t}) - \log(D_{i,t-1})$ as the log dividend growth rate , we rewrite (1) as:

$$h_{i,t} = \log(\exp(\delta_{i,t} - \delta_{i,t+1}) + \exp(\delta_{i,t})) + \Delta d_{i,t} . \tag{2}$$

Note equation (2) is nonlinear in the dividend-price ratio. To get a linear relationship, we can perform a Taylor expansion of $\delta_{i,t+1}$ and $\delta_{i,t}$ around δ_i . It is easy to see that as long as $\delta_{i,t}$ are bounded for all t, the Taylor expansion will always converge, regardless of whether $\delta_{i,t}$ is stationary or not. So we obtain:

$$h_{i,t} \approx \xi_{i,t} , \tag{3a}$$

$$\xi_{i,t} = \delta_{i,t} - \rho_i \delta_{i,t+1} + \Delta d_{i,t} + \kappa_i , \tag{3b}$$

where $\rho_i = 1/(1+\exp(\delta_i))$ and $\kappa_i = -\log(\rho_i) - (1-\rho_i) \delta_i$. Equation (3) says that $h_{i,t}$ can be approximated by $\xi_{i,t}$, which is a linear function of $\delta_{i,t}$, $\delta_{i,t+1}$ and $\Delta d_{i,t}$. In their work, ρ_i is calculated by $\rho_i = \exp(g_i - h_i)$, where g_i is the sample time mean of $\Delta d_{i,t}$ and h_i is the time mean of $h_{i,t}$. [1]

In general, different ρ_i should be used for different assets in (3) to achieve a closest approximation. But since (3) is just a Taylor approximation, and (3) fits C & S' data for price indexes very well for a wide range of ρ , we will use a single ρ for all assets. This is equivalent to performing a Taylor expansion of $\delta_{i,t+1}$ and $\delta_{i,t}$ around δ. With $\rho = 1/(1+\exp(\delta))$ and ρ is calculated by $\rho = \exp(g-h)$, where g is the panel mean of $\Delta d_{i,t}$ and h is the panel mean of $h_{i,t}$ for our data set. It is possible

---

[1] They justified this calculation by using the Gordon formula. See their paper for details about the derivation.

that this practice might create large approximation errors that render our empirical results unreliable. We will provide some evidence, however, that $\xi_{i,t}$ of (3) is a good approximation of $h_{i,t}$.

Using the same ρ for all assets, we write equation (3) as

$$\delta_{i,t} \approx \rho\, \delta_{i,t+1} + h_{i,t} - \Delta d_{i,t} - \kappa' , \tag{4}$$

where $\kappa' = -\log(\rho)-(1-\rho)\delta$. We solve it forward, imposing the terminal condition $\lim_{j-\infty} \rho^j \delta_{i,t+j} = 0$ and denote $\kappa = -\kappa'/(1-\rho)$, we have,

$$\delta_{i,t} \approx \sum_{j=1}^{\infty} \rho^j (h_{i,t+j} - \Delta d_{i,t+j}) + \kappa . \tag{5}$$

According to C & S, "this equation says that the log dividend-price ratio can be written as a discounted value of all future returns less dividend growth rates, discounted at the constant rate ρ less a constant."

So far we have not made any economic assumptions about the determination of asset returns. To impose some restrictions on the behavior of $h_{i,t}$, we assume returns are generated by the following process in a perfect competitive and frictionless asset market:

$$h_{i,t} = r_{i,t} + f_t'\beta_i + \varepsilon_{i,t} , \tag{6}$$

where
$$r_{i,t} = E_t (h_{i,t}) = r_t + q_t'\beta_i . \tag{7}$$

$$E(\varepsilon_{it}) = 0; \qquad E(\varepsilon_{it}\varepsilon_{js}) = \sigma_i^2 \text{ if } i = j \text{ and } s = t ;$$
$$= 0 \quad \text{otherwise,}$$

$$E(f_t) = 0 ; \qquad E(q_t\varepsilon_{i,s}) = E(f_t\varepsilon_{i,s}) = 0 .$$

Here, E_t denotes a rational expectation formed on the information set I_t, which is known to the market at the beginning of period t. r_t and q_t are assumed to be in I_t, and can be thought of as risk free rate and factor premia. The whole economy is driven by r_t and q_t and factor shocks f_t, while the return structure is determined by individual factor loadings β_i and other idiosyncratic disturbances. Model (6) can be thought of as a multi-factor APT model with time-varying risk premia, in which β_i is constant over time but varies across firms. β_i is a vector, (β_{1i}, β_{2i}, ... , β_{Ki}), while K is the number of common risk factors in the market. $r_{i,t}$ denotes the expected one period return. Equation (7) says that the expected return to each security is a linear function of how much systematic risk it bears. Model (6) is more general than the constant-risk-premia APT model tested by Chen(1983) and Roll and Ross(1980). It is similar to the multi-factor latent variables model studied by Campbell(1987), Gibbons and Ferson(1985) and Hansen and Hodrick (1983). But we make no assumptions about the observability of q_t and f_t.

It is worth noting here that although there always exists some β_i *ex post* to make (7) hold, whether it is true or not, that β_i will generally make $\varepsilon_{i,t}$ uncorrelated across securities. Thus, the specification of (7) is restrictive.

If $r_{i,t}$ are observable, the standard way of testing model (6) is to run a *time series* regression of excess return $h_{i,t}$- $r_{i,t}$ on some variables known at the beginning of period t. If the coefficients are jointly significant, then the model is rejected. This is usually called the predictability test. Another way of testing the model is to do a *cross-sectional* regression of $h_{i,t}$ on β_i (assuming it is observable or can be estimated) and other variables known at the beginning of t. If the model is correctly specified, then regressors other than β_i should not have any explanatory power over the structure of $h_{i,t}$. We will call this the "explicability" test. Note the difference between predictability and explicability test is that one examines the movements of return, while the other examines the cross-sectional structure of returns. The framework we use to test the model will be a variant of the explicability test, since β_i is assumed to be *unobservable* in our work.

To derive the dividend ratio model, we combine (5) and (7) and take expectation on the LHS and the RHS of equation (5), conditional on agents' information set I_t at the beginning of period t. We assume $\delta_{i,t}$ and $\Delta d_{i,t-1}$ are in I_t. Thus,

$$\delta_{i,t} \approx \sum_{j=0}^{\infty} \rho^j E_t (h_{i,t+j} - \Delta d_{i,t+j}) + \kappa, \tag{8}$$

where $E_t (h_{i,t+j}) = E_t (r_{t+j}) + E_t (q_{t+j}') \beta_i$, according to equation (7).

Equation (8) is a linearized version of the PVM with time-varying-expected-returns. It is slightly different from C & S' dividend ratio model, because of a different specification of (7). It explains the log dividend-price ratio as an expected discounted value of all future returns adjusted by the dividend growth rate, $h_{i,t+j} - \Delta d_{i,t+j}$. Equation (8) regulates the structure of $\delta_{i,t}$ across firms and the time evolution process of $\delta_{i,t}$ in relation to all future returns and dividend growth rate.

Sometimes it is more convenient to work with a one period model, in which $\delta_{i,t}$, $\delta_{i,t+1}$, $r_{i,t}$ and $\Delta d_{i,t}$ are related. So we take the expectation of both sides of equation (4), conditional on agents' information set I_t at the beginning of period t, and use equation (7), we obtain:

$$\delta_{i,t} = \rho\, E_t\,(\delta_{i,t+1}) + r_t + q_t'\beta_i - E_t(\,\Delta d_{i,t}) - \kappa'. \tag{9}$$

Equation (9) regulates the one period evolution of $\delta_{i,t}$ in relation to its one period ahead expected value and dividend growth. This is useful for deriving some restrictions on the one period evolution process of the dividend-price ratio $\delta_{i,t}$, which will be tested later. It is obvious that we can also derive equation (8) by solving (9) forward and imposing the terminal condition.

Note that equation (9) presumably holds for real variables. But a closer look reveals that it is independent of the price index chosen to deflate the nominal values, because the deflator cancels out on both sides. This gives us a significant advantage over the usual PVM setup, which is not immune to measurement errors of price indexes. Here $\delta_{i,t}$, $r_{i,t}$ and $\Delta d_{i,t}$ are all measured in nominal terms.

III. Test of Model of Expected Returns Using Panel Data

In this section, we will present a framework under which a test of the model of expected return (6) can be performed using panel data. This method is an application of that developed in Mei (1989a).

Our approach uses information conveyed in the historical data about β_i. We run a panel autoregression of returns on lagged returns and other variables. If the model is true, then variables other than return history should have no explanatory power over the structure of returns (i.e., no Granger causality).

Our approach is different from previous work in the following ways: first, we are not subject to the restriction imposed on *time series* regressions that regressors used to predict the excess return must be stationary if conventional asymptotic distribution theory is to apply. This a serious problem because many variables used as regressors, such as price and dividend, have been found to be nonstationary. Since our approach is, in essence, a cross-sectional regression, we do not have this problem.

Secondly, our approach avoids some statistical problems associated with the commonly used two-step approach of studying the expected return model. The two step approach is first to obtain a proxy for beta through a time series regression of returns on some market indexes and then use the proxy as data to run a cross-sectional regression. The substitution of estimated beta for real beta can lead to some serious statistical problems, which was discussed in Miller and Scholes (1972). Our approach is to extract information about beta from past returns and other past variables and just run one panel regression of realized return, $h_{i,t}$, on lagged returns and other variables. Thus, ours is a one-step approach.

Denote $s_t = q_t + f_t$, rewrite (6) as:

$$h_{i,t} = r_t + s_t'\beta_i + \varepsilon_{i,t}. \tag{6}'$$

If we can observe β_i, then, we can just run a cross-sectional regression of $h_{i,t}$ on β_i and other variables $\zeta_{i,t}$ known at the beginning of period t:

$$h_{i,t} = r_t + s_t'\beta_i + \alpha_t' \zeta_{i,t} + \varepsilon_{i,t}. \qquad\qquad i=1,...,\ N \qquad (10)$$

and test: H_0: $\alpha_t = 0$. Unless $\zeta_{i,t}$ is perfectly correlated with β_i , we will not be able to reject H_0 . If it is rejected, we will say $\zeta_{i,t}$ helps explain the structure of future returns and model (6)' is rejected by the data.

Since β_i is unobservable, we have to find some proxy for it. We notice that if (6)' is true, then *past* realized returns $h_{i,s}$ (s<t) carry information about β_i. If we can solve for β_i in terms of past returns and some parameters which are constant across firms, we can plug these information into (6)' and do a autoregression analysis.

For expositional purpose, let us assume, for the moment, that there is only one risk factor(K=1) in the model. To extract information about β_i from past $h_{i,s}$, we take equation (6)' for time period t -1, and solve for β_i in terms of $h_{i,t-1}$:

$$\beta_i = (h_{i,t-1} - r_{t-1} - \varepsilon_{it-1})/ s_{t-1} .$$

Although the RHS error term and parameters are not observable, we note the parameters are *constant across firms* and the error term has nice properties. Substitute this into (6)' for time period t, we obtain:

$$h_{i,t} = r_t + s_t \frac{h_{i,t-1} - r_{t-1} - \varepsilon_{i,t-1}}{s_{t-1}} + \varepsilon_{i,t} \qquad (11)$$

$$(i=1,...,N).$$

Collecting terms, we denote:

$$\psi_{0t} = r_t - \frac{s_t}{s_{t-1}} r_t, \quad \psi_{1t} = \frac{s_t}{s_{t-1}}, \quad \eta_{i,t} = \varepsilon_{i,t} - \frac{s_t}{s_{t-1}} \varepsilon_{i,t-1}, \quad i=1,\cdots,N. \qquad (12)$$

We have:

$$h_{i,t} = \psi_{0t} + \psi_{1t} h_{i,t-1} + \eta_{i,t} . \qquad (13)$$

Thus, if model (6)' is correctly specified, then we should not be able to reject H_0: $\pi_t = 0$ in the following regression:

$$h_{i,t} = \psi_{0t} + \psi_{1t} h_{i,t-1} + \pi_t \zeta_{i,t} + \eta_{i,t} . \qquad (14)$$

It is obvious from (11) and (6)' that the error term $\eta_{i,t}$ is uncorrelated across firms and has a mean of zero. Except for the fact that $h_{i,t-1}$ (and possibly $\zeta_{i,t}$) is correlated with the error term, (14) is a standard linear regression model. If we can find instruments for $h_{i,t-1}$ and $\zeta_{i,t}$, then (14) can be estimated by an instrumental variable regression. (For instance, if we observe $h_{i,t-2}$ and $\zeta_{i,t-2}$, then they can be used as instruments for $h_{i,t-1}$ and $\zeta_{i,t}$.)

In general, if there are K (K>1) risk factors in equation (6), then we need K lagged returns in equation (13) to substitute out β_j. The equivalent of (14) for K (K>1) is

$$h_{i,t} = \psi_{0t} + \sum_{J=1}^{K} \psi_{Jt} h_{i,t-J} + \eta_{i,t} \qquad (15)$$

$$(i=1,...,N).$$

where: $\quad \psi_{0t} = r_t - \sum_{J=1}^{K} \psi_{Jt} r_{i,t-J}$, $\eta_{i,t} = \varepsilon_{i,t} - \sum_{J=1}^{K} \psi_{Jt} \varepsilon_{i,t-J}$.

Thus, η_{it} is a linear function of ε_{it}, $\varepsilon_{it-1},...,$ ε_{it-K} . η_{it} is uncorrelated across firms and has a mean of zero. Parallel to regression (14), if model (6)' is well specified, then, we will not be able to reject H_0: $\pi_t = 0$ in the following regression:

$$h_{i,t} = \psi_{0t} + \sum_{J=1}^{K} \psi_{Jt} h_{i,t-J} + \pi_t \zeta_{i,t} + \eta_{i,t} \qquad (16)$$

Since past returns $h_{i,t-J}$ (J=1,...,K) (and possibly $\zeta_{i,t}$) are correlated with the error term η_{it} through correlation with $\varepsilon_{it-1},...,$ ε_{it-K}, equation (16) must be estimated by an instrumental variables regression. $h_{i,t-J}$ (J<t-K) and other variables in information set I_{t-K} qualify to be instruments. We have employed a three-stage-least-square (3SLS) estimation technique, developed by H, N & R, that will allow us to estimate equation (16) for many time periods simultaneously. The technical details of the procedure is given in Appendix I. Here we just offer some intuitive explanation.

The estimation procedure is quite similar to that of the 3SLS method used in the estimation of simultaneous equations. In the first stage, OLS is used to find the appropriate instruments for $h_{i,t-J}$ (J=1,...,K) and $\zeta_{i,t}$. In the second stage, equation (16) is estimated by an instrumental variable regression for each time period, ignoring the serial correlation and heteroskedasticity of the error term. During the third stage, the residuals from the regression of the second stage are used to calculate a White (1980) variance-covariance matrix of the error terms and a generalized least squares technique is used to obtain a more efficient estimate of equation (16) for all time periods. The estimate will be consistent despite the existence of serial correlation and heteroskedasticity of the error term.

To test restrictions such as $\pi_t = 0$ and how many lags we should use in (16), we employ a procedure similar to the Chow test. The strategy is first to estimate the *unrestricted* model and the *restricted* model and then calculate the difference in their sum of squared residuals, Q_U and Q_R. If the restrictions do not hold, then the difference($L = Q_R - Q_U$) will be large, indicating a rejection of the hypothesis. See Appendix I for details.

The choice of instruments for $h_{i,t-J}$ (J=1,...,K) and $\zeta_{i,t}$ can be crucial in a small sample study, since it affects the estimation efficiency. For equation (16), we choose to use $h_{i,t-J}$ (J=K+1,..., 2K+1) and lagged $\zeta_{i,t}$ in information set I_{t-K} as instruments, because they are *cross-sectionally* correlated with $h_{i,t-J}$ and $\zeta_{i,t}$, but not with the error term, $\eta_{i,t}$.

IV. Vector Autoregression and the Dividend Ratio Model

Although we have presented a framework in Part III under which the model of one-period expected return can be tested, complementary work is necessary because this test has some pitfalls. First, as argued by Shiller (1984) and Summers (1986), single period return regressions have low statistical power in detecting minor but long-lived deviations of returns from the model. Secondly, even if the regression results reject the return model, we still do not know how far the stock price would deviate from its "fundamental values". This point was made forcefully by Campbell and Shiller (1987,1988a,1988b). In what follows, we assume the panel data is generated by a stable, linear stochastic process. We will study the restriction imposed on the process by the dividend ratio model. We hope this study can be a step towards avoiding the above pitfalls.

A. Vector Autoregressive Process

Assume the economy is characterized by a vector of state variables y_t. At the beginning of time t, market participants observe y_t and its past history, so their information set is $I_t = \{ y_t , y_{t-1} , ... \}$. Let x_t be the vector of variables that is a subset of y_t, which we econometricians can observe. Our information set, H_t, is $\{ x_t , x_{t-1} , ... \}$. Here we choose x_t to be $\{ \delta_{1,t} , \Delta d_{1,t-1}; \delta_{2,t} , \Delta d_{2,t-1}; ... ; \delta_{N,t}, \Delta d_{N,t-1} \}$. N is the number of securities in our data set. We lag the growth of dividend one period to make sure it is known to us at the beginning of t .

We assume that $\{ \delta_{i,t} , \Delta d_{i,t-1} \}$ evolve according to the following VAR process with p-lags:

$$\delta_{i,t} = a_{0t} + \sum_{J=1}^{P} a_{Jt}\, \delta_{i,t-J} + \sum_{J=1}^{P} b_{Jt}\, \Delta d_{i,t-J-1} + \varphi_t \beta_i + u_{i,t} \qquad (17)$$

$$\Delta d_{i,t-1} = c_{0t} + \sum_{J=1}^{P} c_{Jt}\, \delta_{i,t-J} + \sum_{J=1}^{P} d_{Jt}\, \Delta d_{i,t-J-1} + \tau_t \beta_i + v_{i,t} \qquad (18)$$

$$(i=1,...,N;\ t = (p+2),...,T),$$

$$E(\delta_{i,s}\, u_{i,t}) = E(\Delta d_{i,s-1}\, u_{i,t}) = 0; \quad E(\delta_{i,s}\, v_{i,t}) = E(\Delta d_{i,s-1}\, v_{i,t}) = 0; \quad (s<t)$$

$$E(u_{i,s}\, u_{j,t}) = E(v_{i,s}\, v_{j,t}) = 0. \qquad (i \neq j) \qquad (19)$$

Here, the coefficients are allow to vary over time, but not across securities. They are assumed to be known to the market participants at the beginning of time t. φ_t and τ_t are vectors of unspecified economic variables that determine how big an effect will the individual effects (firm risk features) have on the dividend-price ratio and the dividend growth at time t.

In equation (17) and (18), the error terms $u_{i,t}$ and $v_{j,t}$ are assumed to be white noise. No correlation of errors among securities is allowed. The variance of $u_{i,t}$ and $v_{j,t}$ could vary across securities, but not over time. No assumption is made about the correlation between $u_{i,t}$ and $v_{i,t}$. Thus, (17) and (18) allow two kinds of individual heterogeneity, the multiple individual effects associated with firms' risk features and cross-sectional heteroskedasticity.

Again, by allowing the coefficients in (17) and (18) to vary over time, we can use nominal variables instead of real ones, because the price deflator will be "absorbed" in the time-varying coefficients.

One difficulty involved in estimating (17) and (18) directly is that the individual risk feature is not observable. By taking the advantage of panel study, we can completely ignor the unobservability problems, as long as betas are time invariant.

We use the same method as we did in Part III to extract information about β_i conveyed in past $\delta_{i,s}$ and $\Delta d_{i,s-1}$. We take equation (17) from time period t-1 to t-K and stack them together as a system of linear equations with β_i being the unknown variable.(see equation (14) for a hint.) We then solve for β_i in terms of $\delta_{i,s}$ and $\Delta d_{i,s-1}$ (s=t-1~t-K-p) and substitute it into equation (17) *for time period t*, and collect terms, we obtain a VAR process with p+K lags(do the same for equation (18)) :

$$\delta_{i,t} = \beta_{0t} + \sum_{J=1}^{p+K} \beta_{Jt}\delta_{i,t-J} + \sum_{J=1}^{p+K} \gamma_{Jt}\Delta d_{i,t-J-1} + \varpi_{i,t} \qquad (20)$$

$$\Delta d_{i,t-1} = \phi_{0t} + \sum_{J=1}^{p+K} \phi_{Jt}\delta_{i,t-J} + \sum_{J=1}^{p+K} \lambda_{Jt}\Delta d_{i,t-J-1} + \upsilon_{i,t} \qquad (21)$$

$$(i=1,...,N; t=(p+K+2),...,T),$$

where $\varpi_{i,t}$ is a linear function of $u_{i,t}$, $u_{i,t-1}$, ..., $u_{i,t-K}$ and $\upsilon_{i,t}$ is a linear combination of $v_{i,t}$, $v_{i,t-1}$, ..., $v_{i,t-K}$. Parallel to the orthogonality conditions listed in (19), we can derive the following conditions:

$$E(\delta_{i,s}\,\varpi_{i,t}) = E(\Delta d_{i,s-1}\,\varpi_{i,t}) = 0; \quad E(\delta_{i,s}\,\upsilon_{i,t}) = E(\Delta d_{i,s-1}\,\upsilon_{i,t}) = 0; \quad (s<t-K)$$

$$E(\varpi_{i,s}\,\varpi_{j,t}) = E(\upsilon_{i,s}\,\upsilon_{j,t}) = 0, \qquad (i \neq j) \qquad (22)$$

which means that $\delta_{i,s}$ and $\Delta d_{i,s-1}$ (s<t-K) qualify to be instruments for estimating (20) and (21), Since they are not correlated with the error terms $\varpi_{i,t}$ and $\upsilon_{i,t}$.

The intercept and lagged coefficients in (20) are functions of current and past a_{Jt}, b_{Jt} and ϕ_t in (17). To conserve space, the transformation equations are omitted. Although we can identify the coefficients of (17) and (18) from the estimates of those of (20) and (21) under certain conditions, they are quite tedious and often of no particular interest. One special case is non-Granger causality(i.e. $b_{Jt}=0$, $c_{Jt}=0$, $J=1 \sim p$). But this can be easily tested on the estimates of (20) and (21), since non-Granger causality of (17) and (18)($b_{Jt}=0$, $c_{Jt}=0$) imply the same property of (20) and (21)($\gamma_{Jt}=0$, $\phi_{Jt}=0$), because there will be no $\Delta d_{i,s-1}$ terms in equation (20), unless there are $\Delta d_{i,s-1}$ terms in equation (17).

As pointed out by C & S, one weak restriction the dividend-ratio model imposes on the coefficients of the VAR process is that $\delta_{i,t}$ should Granger cause $\Delta d_{i,t-1}$. This is because the market participants know more information about the future dividend growth than we econometricians, and they will incorporate this additional information when they use equation (8) to determine the value of $\delta_{i,t}$. Thus $\delta_{i,t}$ should have extra explanatory power over the historical dividend data for explaining the cross-sectional difference in future dividend growth. That is to say the coefficient c_{Jt} in (18) and ϕ_{Jt} in (21) should generally be non-zero. A formal procedure is designed to test this hypothesis.

In their paper, C & S also derived a strong constraint imposed on the parameters of the VAR process for time series data under the assumption of constant parameters and observability of expected returns *ex post*. We have generalized their result by dropping the observability assumption.[2] Although the empirical test of the strong constraints should be very interesting, in this paper,

---

[2] Interested reader may see Mei(1989b) for derivation of the strong constraint and discussion of some difficulties involved in estimation and testing.

we present a much simpler alternative test for the dividend model.

B. An Alternative Test of the Dividend- Ratio Model

In this section, we will derive the constraints imposed on a vector autoregression of $\delta_{i,t}$ by equation (9). As in Part III, we begin with a one risk factor model, then generalize.

Assume (17) and (18) are well specified and market participants have one period perfect foresight of the lagged coefficients and the intercept , then

$$\delta_{i,t+1} = E_t(\delta_{i,t+1}) + (\varphi_{t+1} - E_t(\varphi_{t+1}))\beta_i + u_{i,t+1}, \qquad (23)$$

$$\Delta d_{i,t} = E_t(\Delta d_{i,t}) + (\tau_{t+1} - E_t(\tau_{t+1}))\beta_i + v_{i,t+1}. \qquad (24)$$

Combining equation (9) with (23) and (24), denote $m_{t+1} = \varphi_{t+1} - E_t(\varphi_{t+1})$, and $n_{t+1} = \tau_{t+1} - E_t(\tau_{t+1})$, we obtain,

$$\delta_{i,t+1} = -\rho^{-1}(r_t - \kappa') - \rho^{-1}(q_t - \rho\, m_{t+1} + n_{t+1})\beta_i + \rho^{-1}\delta_{i,t}$$

$$+ \rho^{-1}\Delta d_{i,t} + u_{i,t+1} - \rho^{-1}v_{i,t+1}. \qquad (25)$$

To get rid of the β_i term in equation (25), we take equation (25) *for time period t* and solve for β_i in terms of $\delta_{i,t}$, $\delta_{i,t-1}$ and $\Delta d_{i,t-1}$, then substitute them for β_i in equation (25) and collect terms, we have

$$\delta_{i,t+1} = e_t + (\rho^{-1} + g_t)\delta_{i,t} - \rho^{-1}g_t\delta_{i,t-1} + \rho^{-1}\Delta d_{i,t} - \rho^{-1}g_t\Delta d_{i,t-1} + \mu_{i,t+1} \quad (26)$$

where $g_t = (q_t - \rho\, m_{t+1} + n_{t+1})/(q_{t-1} - \rho\, m_t + n_t)$, $e_t = -\rho^{-1}(r_t - \kappa') + \rho^{-1}g_t(r_{t-1} - \kappa')$ and $\mu_{i,t+1} = u_{i,t+1} - \rho^{-1}v_{i,t+1} - g_t(u_{i,t} - \rho^{-1}v_{i,t})$. Notice $\Delta d_{i,t}$, $\Delta d_{i,t-1}$ and $\delta_{i,t}$ are correlated with the error term $\mu_{i,t+1}$. From (26), we can see that the coefficients of the autoregression is constrained in certain ways if equation (23) and (24) and model (9) hold. This leads us to run a panel regression of (26) and test these constraints.

More specifically, we first use $\delta_{i,s}$ and $\Delta d_{i,s-1}$ ($s \leq t-1$) as instruments to estimate:

$$\delta_{i,t+1} = e_t + \eta_{0t}\delta_{i,t} + \eta_{1t}\delta_{i,t-1} + \theta_{0t}\Delta d_{i,t} + \theta_{1t}\Delta d_{i,t-1} + \mu_{i,t+1} \qquad (27)$$

Next, we will perform a hypothesis testing based on equation (26). If (26) is true, then we will not be able to reject:

$$H_0: \eta_{1t} = \theta_{1t}, (\theta_{0t} - \eta_{0t})\, \theta_{0t} - \theta_{1t} = 0. \tag{28}$$

We should emphasis here that (27) is estimated essentially by a cross-sectional GLS regression. But we have employed a 3SLS method, as in Part III, which allows us to exploit the information contained in the serial correlated error terms and make adjustment for heteroskedasticity.

It is important to point out here that the test of (28) does not depend on the assumption that lagged coefficients and individual effects are constant over time. All we need is one period foresight of the market participants on these parameters with respect to the lagged coefficients in (17) and (18).

If there are K-risk factors in the linear factor model (6), as well as in equation (9), then we can derive a similar results as of (26) to (28) from equation (25). The equivalent of (26) here is[3]

$$\delta_{i,t+1} = e_t + \sum_{J=0}^{K-1} \{ (\rho^{-1} g_{Jt} - g_{J+1,t}) \delta_{i,t-J} + \rho^{-1} g_{Jt} \Delta d_{i,t-J} \}$$

$$+ \rho^{-1} g_{Kt} \delta_{i,t-K} + \rho^{-1} g_{Kt} \Delta d_{i,t-K} + \mu_{i,t+1}, \tag{29}$$

where $g_{0t} = 1$, and g_{Jt} are free parameters. We also know that $\mu_{i,t+1}$ is a linear function of $u_{i,t+1}$ $v_{i,t+1}$,..., and $u_{i,t-K+1}$, $v_{i,t-K+1}$. Thus all RHS variables are correlated with error term except $\delta_{i,t-K}$. It is obvious here that $\delta_{i,s}$ and $\Delta d_{i,s-1}$ ($s \leq t-K$) qualify to be instruments for regression. Write (29) as:

$$\delta_{i,t+1} = f_t + \sum_{J=0}^{K} \{ \eta_{Jt} \delta_{i,t-J} + \theta_{Jt} \Delta d_{i,t-J} \} + \mu_{i,t+1} \tag{30}$$

We can see from (29) that the parameters of (30) are subject to the following K+1 constraints:

_____

[3]Appendix II derives the result shown here.

$$H_0:\ \eta_{Kt} = \theta_{Kt}\ ,\ (\ \theta_{Jt} - \eta_{Jt})\ \theta_{0t} - \theta_{J+1,t} = 0 \qquad (J=0\sim K\text{-}1). \qquad (31)$$

Hypothesis (31) defines a set of K+1 nonlinear restrictions on the coefficients of equation (30) for each period's regression. A nonlinear Wald test can be constructed to see if the data reject (28) or (31). Using C & S' notation, if we write the estimated coefficients vector of (30) as γ, the estimated variance-covariance matrix of the vector as Θ, and the vector of deviations from (31) as λ, then the Wald test statistic is:

$$W = \lambda\ '\ [\partial\lambda/\partial\gamma\ '\ \Theta\ \partial\lambda/\partial\gamma\ ]^{-1}\ \lambda. \qquad (32)$$

Under the null hypothesis, it is distributed χ^2 with degrees of freedom equal to the number of restrictions, which is K+1.

If we wish to do a joint test that (31) is true for all years estimated, then we can just use (32) to construct a Wald-statistic which includes coefficients of equation (30) for all time periods. Its degrees of freedom will equal to K+1 times the number of years of which (30) is estimated. The purpose of doing this test is to see whether equation (9) holds for all years estimated. Since (8) is derived from assuming (9) is true for all future time periods and the terminal condition, it is quite possible that the market can deviate greatly from (8) while only slightly from (9). By doing a joint test of (31), we might be able to detect some minor but recurring deviations of the dividend-price ratio from equation (9).

V. Data Description and Empirical results

A. About the Data

The main data set used here is the Compustat Annual Industrial File. One advantage of working with this file is that it readily provides us with annually adjusted dividend and closing price data. We choose to work with annual data because firms do not change their dividend policy often. Those industrial companies, which were included in the S&P 400 index and existed for the whole sample period and always paid a positive annual dividend, are selected into the panel. We are aware that this selection process may introduce survival bias to our empirical results.

We use the absolute closing price per share from last year for P_t and the cash dividend per share whose ex-dividend dates occurred during the year for D_t. Both are adjusted for all stock splits and stock dividends that occurred during the year. They are further adjusted by the Cumulative Adjustment Factor to place them on the same terms as the latest share units. The constructed data set has been checked against the Moody's Handbook for Common Stocks for errors. They match very well. Table 1 gives some further details about the data structure.

In Table 2, we present some summary statistics about the panel data. The ρ used in calculating for ξ_{it} is 0.9757, which is estimated by the panel mean of $\Delta d_{i,t}$ and $h_{i,t}$ provided in panel B of Table 2. Panel D provides the overall (panel) correlation coefficient between $h_{i,t}$ and $\xi_{i,t}$, which is 0.9944, suggesting that these two variables are highly correlated and the approximation error is small. The comparison of sample mean of $h_{i,t}$ and $\xi_{i,t}$ for each year in panel A also indicates that the approximation error is probably quite small.

B. Estimation and Testing

Using the panel data set constructed from the Compustat Annual Industrial File, we estimate equation (16), (20) and (21) and (30). We conduct test for minimum lag length, Granger causality and restrictions on the coefficients of (30) imposed by the dividend-ratio model. We also compared our results against the work by C & S.

Our strategy is to begin by specifying a quite long initial lag length , based on previous empirical work by other authors and the capacity of our data set, and use the test procedure described in Appendix I to find a minimum lag length. Then we test the model conditional on several specification of lag length. We start with K=6 in regression of (16), which allow the model to have at most 6 risk factors. (Roll and Ross(1980) found 3-4 factors. Chen(1983) assumed five factors.) We begin estimating equation (20) and (21) with p+K=6 as well, which we think can incorporate the fact that there are roughly 3-4 risk factors in the market and we also allow the initial VAR process of (17) and (18) to have its own lag length of p=1-2.

Although it is desirable to begin with a even longer initial lag length, that raises problems in practice. The size of the weighting matrix Ω in the 3SLS will increase very rapidly with increase in the initial lag length and the number of time period estimated. For example, if the number of years estimated for (20) is five and p+K=6 and we use fifteen instrumental variables for each year, the size of Ω will be 75 x 75. As is well known, standard numerical procedure for matrix inversion may not give us reliable answer when the matrix to be inverted gets too large. We estimate the above equations for the years of 1982-1987. The results are presented from Table 3 to Table 12.

1) Test of Expected Return Model(16)

We display regression results for equation (16) in Table 3 with $\delta_{i,t}$ being $\zeta_{i,t}$. We do not use $\delta_{i,t}$ and $\Delta d_{i,t-1}$ together because this will introduce multicollinearity into the regression due to identity (4). We estimate (16) first and then replace $h_{i,t}$ with the approximate return $\xi_{i,t}$. If the approximation error is small, the regression results should be very similar. We report them in Table 3 and 5, respectively.

The first column of Table 3 specifies lag length and explanatory variables in the regression. The second column gives the generalized sum of squared residuals, Q, corresponding to each specification. To find the minimum lag length, we check each specification of lag length against the specification above it in the table, which contains one more lag. For example, we calculate $L_{(K=2)}$ $=Q_{(K=2)}-Q_{(K=3)} = 53.057-40.303=12.754$. The L-value measures the generalized sum of squard residuals reduced by the introduction of one more lag into the regression. If the specification is correct, then L follows χ^2 distribution with degrees of freedom given by the fourth column. The last column presents the significance level at which the specification is rejected.

As lines two to four of panel A in Table 3 show, we can not reject the hypothesis that equation (16) might have 3-5 lags. For example, the L value of the second line in panel A (9.350) tells us that we can not reject K=5 at any significance level less than 9%(P=0.095). From line five of panel A, we see that the hypothesis K=2 is strongly rejected(P=0.025), indicating that equation (16) has at least 3 lags(or the market has at least three common risk factors).

Table 4 presents estimates of equation (16) with $h_{i,s}$ and $\delta_{i,s}$ used as regressors for K=3. One can see that there are a few coefficients of lag 3 which are statistically significant. This confirms our results from Table 3. Also by looking at estimates of the equation with longer lags, such as K=6, we find that the estimated coefficients for long lags usually are not significant.[4]

Since we can not tell precisely how many lags there are in equation (16), we will test the non-Granger causality condition(H_0: $\pi_t=0$) based on all possible specification of lag length in our regression. In panel B of Table 3, we calculate the L-statistic as the difference between the generalized sum of squard residuals of the restricted ($\pi_t=0$) and the unrestricted system. For example, $L_{(K=2,R)}$ = $Q_{(K=2,R)}$-$Q_{(K=2)}$ = 75.700 - 53.057 = 22.643. As before, the last two columns give the degrees of freedom and the significance level.

From lines one to five of panel B in Table 3, we can see that the condition ($\pi_t=0$) is strongly rejected for K=2 and 5 and weakly rejected for K=3 and 4, implying a weak rejection of the inexplicability property of model (6) for K ≤ 5. Thus, we can interpret the results as the rejection of the APT model with time-varying risk premia by our data for K ≤ 5. [5] But the model is not rejected for K=6.

Comparing Table 3 and 5, we can see that the results given are very close. We have also compared their regression coefficients, which shows a great agreement as well.[6] This confirms that the approximation error of $\xi_{i,t}$ to $h_{i,t}$ is small. (Column Q is deleted in Table 5 for conserving space.)

----

[4],[6]These regression results can be obtained from the author upon request.
[5]Note that our rejection of the APT model (6) for K ≤ 5 does not necessarily falsify our results about the minimum number of risk factors in the model. An intuitive reason is that it needs four or five betas in model (6) to explain the return structure well but the model may still fail to explain all the variation in returns across firms.

Regression results for equation (16) with $\Delta d_{i,t-1}$ being $\zeta_{i,t}$ are presented in Table 6. Test of minimum lag length in panel A suggests there are at least 4 lags in equation (16), indicating the existence of at least 4 risk factors in the market.

Conditional on K=2,3,4,5 and 6, we performed the test of $\Delta d_{i,t-1}$ Granger causing $h_{i,t}$ in panel B. We find $\Delta d_{i,t-1}$ does not have significant explanatory power when K=2 and 6, but has some power when K=3,4 and 5. Comparing to what we found in Table 3, we can see that $\delta_{i,t}$ has a little more power on average in explaining the structure of future returns than $\Delta d_{i,t-1}$ for $K \leq 5$. This to some extent agrees with several previous studies(such as Fama and French(1988), Flood, Hodrick and Kaplan(1986), Porterba and Summers(1987)), which assert that variables including price information usually contain more information about future return than those without it.

2). The Dividend-Price Ratio Equation (20)

Table 7 presents results for the test of H_0: $\gamma_{Jt}=0$ for equation(20). The test of lag length is omitted here to conserve space. We just report that equation (20) needs at least 3 lags. Table 9 gives estimates of equation (20) with m=p+K=3. As lines one and two of Table 7 show, we can reject H_0:$\gamma_{Jt}=0$ at significance level of 0.0009 and 0.0175, conditional on m =3 and 4. So past dividend growth rates seem to have a impact on the structure of dividend-price ratios across firms. But this result is not robust with respect to the specification of lag length m.

3). The Dividend Growth Equation(21)

Our test for minimum lag length indicates that equation (21) needs at least 3 lags, with the results now leaning more towards 4 or 5 lags. So the test of lag length of (20) and (21) give us a consistent picture about how many lags should be in the system of (20) and (21). Table 9 also gives the estimates of equation(21) with p+K=3. One can see that there are more coefficients of lag 3 which are statistically significant.

Table 7 presents results for the test of H_0: $\phi_{Jt}=0$ for equation(21). According to C & S, information about future dividend changes, which we econometricians do not observe, has been incorporated into the dividend-price ratio by market participants. Thus, $\delta_{i,s}$ carries information about dividend growth. From lines one to two, we have some empirical evidence supporting their argument. Past log dividend-price ratios do explain future dividend changes. But this explanatory power seems to diminish when more lagged dividend-growth variables are introduced into equation (21).

Before we go on to the estimation and testing of equation (30), it is interesting to compare our estimates with C & S' results. if we both estimate a one-lag VAR with constant coefficients under the assumption of constant-expected-returns (β_i =0,r_t is constant in (7)). Although our previous test strongly rejects this version, it is still informative to compare the results. We expect the two estimates to be quite close, because in theory, price indexes should represent major properties of individual securities. From Table 10, we can see that the results are similar in some respects.

4). The Dividend-Ratio Model Test Equation(30)

As in the previous sections, we begin here by testing the minimum lag length of the model. We find that the equation has a minimum lag length of three, which indicates that K $\geq$2.

In Table 11, we present estimates of equation (30), assuming K=2. If equation (29) is true, we expect the coefficients of $\Delta d_{i,t-1}$ (ρ^{-1}) to be greater than one but close to unity. In reality, they are not always greater than one. But three out of five of them are greater than one and fairly close to one.

To formally test the hypothesis of (31), we calculate the Wald-test statistic for each year and for the entire estimation period(1983-1987). The results are given in Table 12. Since we can not tell precisely what K is in the equation, we give the Wald-statistics for K=2,3,4 and 5. From Table 12, we can see that the dividend ratio model is rejected for K=2 and 3, but not for K=4 and 5.

Since the dividend ratio model is derived from the expected return model, this rejection for K $\leq$ 3 should not be surprising, because our previous test of equation (16) rejects the expected return model for K $\leq$ 5. What is interesting is that the test fails to reject the dividend ratio model for K $\geq$ 4. This might suggest that the parametric test of hypothesis (31) have less power in detecting deviation of returns from the expected return model than single-period return regression test.

But it could also indicate that the dividend ratio model can still hold even if there is some deviation of returns from the expected return model. Since the number of risk factors in the market determines how variable the expected return might be, we see that the more variable the expected return, the less likely the dividend ratio model be rejected. If this is truly the case, then we might be able to save the PVM through further study of variable expected return model and need not resort to models of "rational bubbles" and "fads".

VI. Conclusions

In this paper, we have developed a new approach to the analysis of a model of expected returns and its relationship with the dividend-price ratio of corporate stocks. Beginning with a linear factor model for expected returns, we have studied whether returns are "explicable" through a panel regression. To obtain a framework for analyzing the implication of the return model on the movements and structure of stock prices, we have employed the dividend ratio model developed by Campbell & Shiller and tested the restrictions it imposes on the VAR process which we assume to generate the panel data.

We have found that the data reject the linear factor model as a model of expected returns for an efficient capital market if the number of factors, K, is less than six. The data also reject the linearized version of the PVM if the number of factors in the economy is less than three. We have some evidence that the log dividend-price ratio moves with the rationally expected future growth in dividends, since the log dividend-price ratios Granger cause the dividend growth rates. This means the weak restriction of the dividend ratio model imposed on the VAR process is not rejected.

These conclusions are drawn based on a methodology that is significantly more general and robust than any previous studies. First, we allow time varying expected returns and different risk features for each firm. Our model incorporates many models used by other authors as special case, such as Campbell and Shiller (1988b) and West (1987). Secondly, we have introduced a powerful method of panel regression into the study of the present value model, which has the potential to allow us to study both the movements and structure of share prices.

Thirdly, because of the relative simplicity of cross-sectional regression, which is the essence of panel study, our approach is free from many statistical problems associated with time series study. For instance, the unit-root problem and the problem of estimation bias due to small samples. See Flavin (1983), Kleidon (1986) and Stambaugh (1986) for an evaluation of these problems.

However, our study has some limitations: Because of some unsolved statistical problems, our approach fails in general to derive numerical values for the theoretical movements of dividend-price ratio as implied by the dividend ratio model. Thus we can not compare the actual values of dividend-price ratio with its theoretical values and study their volatility.

Our results on the dividend ratio model rely on the accuracy of the Taylor approximation of the log return on stocks. According to our empirical study, the approximation error seems to be small.

The statistical power of our parametric test is also an important issue that needs further study.

Reference

Black, Fisher and Myron Scholes, 1974, "The Effects of Dividend Yield and Dividend Policy on Common Stock Price and Returns", Journal of Financial Economics, 1, 1-22.

Campbell, John Y., 1987, "Stock Returns and the Term Structure", Journal of Financial Economics, 18, 373-399.

Campbell, John Y. and Robert Shiller, 1987, "Cointegration and Tests of Present Value Models," Journal of Political Economy, 95, 1062-1088.

Campbell, John Y. and Robert Shiller, 1988a, "Stock Prices, Earnings, and Expected Dividends", Journal of Finance, 43, 611-676.

Campbell, John Y. and Robert Shiller, 1988b,"The Dividend Price Ratio and Expectation of Future Dividends and Discount Factors", NBER Working Paper NO. 2100.

Chamberlain, Gary, 1982, "Multivariate Regression Models for Panel Data", Journal of Econometrics, 18, 5-46.

Fama, Eugene F. and Kenneth R. French, 1988, "Permanent and Temporary Components of Stock Prices", Journal Political Economy, 96, 246-273.

Flavin, Marjorie A., 1983, "Excess Volatility in Financial Markets: A Reassessment of the Empirical Evidence", Journal Political Economy, 91, 929-956.

Flood, Robert P., Robert J. Hodrick, and Paul Kaplan, 1986, "An Evaluation of the Recent Evidence on Stock Market Bubbles", NBER Working Paper No. 1971.

French, Kenneth R., William G. Schwert, and Robert F. Stambaugh, 1987, " Expected Stock Returns and Volatility", Journal of Financial Economics, 19, 3-29.

Gibbons, Michael R. and Wayne Ferson, 1985, "Testing Asset Pricing Models with Changing Expectations and an Unobservable Market Portfolio", Journal of Financial Economics, 14, 217-236.

Hansen, Lars P. and Robert J. Hodrick, 1983, "Risk Averse Speculation in the Forward Foreign Exchange Market: An Econometric Analysis of Linear Models", in Jacob A. Frenkel, ed.,"Exchange Rates and International Macro-economics", University of Chicago Press.

Holtz-Eakin, Douglas , Whitney Newey and Harvey Rosen, 1988 ,"Estimating Vector Autoregressions with Panel Data", Econometrica, 56,1371-1395.

Keim, Donald B. and Robert F. Stambaugh, 1986, "Predicting Returns in the Stock and Bond Markets", Journal of Financial Economics, 17,357-390.

Kleidon, Allan W. 1986, "Variance Bound Tests and Stock Price Valuation Models", Journal Political Economy, 94, 953-1001.

LeRoy, Stephen F. and Richard D. Porter, 1981,"The Present Value Relation:

Tests based on Implied Variance Bounds", Econometrica, 49, 97-113.

Mankiw, N. Gregory, David Romer, and Matthew D. Shapiro, 1985, "An Unbiased Reexamination of Stock Market Volatility", Journal of Finance, 40, 677-687.

Miller, Merton H. and Myron Scholes, 1972, "Rates of Return in Relation to Risk: A Re-examination of Some Recent Findings." in Michael C. Jensen, ed. *Studies in the Theory of Capital Markets.*. New YorK, Praeger.

Mei, Jianping, 1989a, "Do We Have to Know Betas ? An Autoregressive Method for Testing the APT." Financial Research Working Paper, # 107, Princeton University.

Mei, Jianping, 1989b, "A Short Note on a Strong Restriction Imposed on a VAR Process by the Dividend Ratio Model." Unpublished Paper, Princeton University.

Newey, Whitney K. and Kenneth D. West, 1987, "A simple, Positive Definite, Heteroskedasticity and Autocorrelation Consistent Covariance Matrix", Econometrica, 55, 703-708.

Poterba, James M. and Lawrence H. Summers, 1986, "The Persistence of Volatility and Stock Market Fluctuations",American Economic Review, 76, 1142-1151.

Poterba, James M. and Lawrence H. Summers, 1987, "Mean Reversion in Stock Prices: Evidence and Implications", Working Paper, Harvard University.

Roll, Richard and Stephen A. Ross, 1980, "An Empirical Investigation of the Arbitrage Pricing Theory", Journal of Finance, 35, 1073-1103.

Shiller, Robert J. , 1981, "Do Stock Prices Move Too Much to be Justified by Subsequent Changes in Dividends ?", American Economic Review, 71, 421-436.

Shiller, Robert J. , 1984, "Stock Price and Social Dynamics", Brookings papers on Economic Activity, 457-498.

Stambaugh, Robert F., 1986, "Bias in Regressions with Lagged Stochastic Regressors", unpublished paper, Graduate School of Business, University of Chicago.

Summers, Lawrence H. 1986, "Does the Stock Market Rationally Reflect Fundamental Values ?", Journal of Finance, 41, 591-601.

West , Kenneth D., 1987,"A Specification Test for Speculative Bubbles", Quarterly Journal of Economics, 102, 553-580.

West , Kenneth D., 1988,"Dividend Innovations and Stock Price Volatility", Econometrica, 56, 37-61.

White, Halbert ,1980,"A Heteroskedasticity-consistent Covariance Matrix Estimator and a Direct Test for Heterokedasticity", Econometrica, 48, 817-838.

Appendix I

In what follows, we present a framework under which autoregression (16), (20), (21) and (30) can be estimated and the restrictions tested. We will use (20) as an example. Using H, N & R's notation, we write:

$$Y_t = (\delta_{1,t}, \delta_{2,t}, \dots \delta_{N,t})' \qquad X_t = (\Delta d_{1,t-1}, \Delta d_{2,t-1}, \dots, \Delta d_{N,t-1})'$$

as Nx1 vectors of observations for a given time period t .

Denote "m" to be the total number of lags used in the autoregression. (In the case of (16), m=K. In (20) and (21), m=p+K. m=K+1 in (30).) Let $W_t = (e, Y_{t-1},\dots, Y_{t-m}, X_{t-1}, \dots, X_{t-m})$. They are the RHS variables of (20). e is a Nx1 vector of ones.

Let $U_t = (\varpi_{1,t}, \varpi_{2,t}, \dots, \varpi_{N,t})'$ be the transformed error terms, and let $B_t = (\beta_{0t}, \beta_{1t}, \dots \beta_{mt}, \gamma_{1t}, \dots \gamma_{mt})'$. Then equation (20) can be written as:

$$Y_t = W_t B_t + U_t. \tag{A1}$$

$$(t = m+1,\dots, T)$$

To combine equation (A1) over time into system of equations, we "stack" equation (A1) by time and denote:

$$Y = (Y_{m+1}',\dots, Y_T')' ; \qquad ((T-m)Nx1)$$

$$B = (B_{m+1}',\dots, B_T')' ; \qquad ((T-m)(2m+1)x1)$$

$$U = (U_{m+1}',\dots, U_T')' ; \qquad ((T-m)Nx1)$$

$$W = \text{diag} (W_{m+1}',\dots, W_T') ; \qquad ((T-m)Nx(T-m)(2m+1))$$

where diag $(W_{m+1}',\dots, W_T')$ denotes a block diagonal matrix with $W_{m+1}',\dots, W_T'$ placed on the diagonal. Thus equation (20) can be written as :

$$Y = WB + U .\tag{A2}$$

From the orthogonality condition (22), it is clear that for equation (A1), the following variables qualify for instrumental variables:

$$Z_t = (e,\ Y_{t-K-1},...,\ Y_1,\ X_{t-K-1},...,\ X_1) .$$

Letting $Z = \mathrm{diag}\ (Z_{m+1}',...,\ Z_T')$ and using the 3SLS estimation method given by H, N& R , we can get   a consistent estimate of B:

$$\hat{B} = [W'Z(\tilde{\Omega})^{-1}Z'W]^{-1}\ W'Z(\tilde{\Omega})^{-1}Z'Y\tag{A3}$$

in which Ω is the covariance matrix of $Z'U$.[*]

The estimate of B given by (A3) has taken into consideration the correlation of the RHS variables with the error terms as well as the heteroskedasticity and the serial correlation of errors over time. It is an extension of White's(1980) heteroskedasticity consistent estimator. In this paper, we estimate equation (16), (20), (21) and (30) separately. With a larger computer capacity and better matrix inversion technology, we could improve the estimate efficiency by *jointly* estimating several sets of equations. In doing so, we might be able to utilize the information contained in the correlation of errors of different set of equations, such as $\varpi_{i,t}$ and $\upsilon_{i,t}$ in equation (20) and (21).

Equation (16), (21) and (30) can be estimated with essentially the same procedure.

Note that the test of how many lags should be in the autoregressive process and the test of the non-Granger causality can all be treated as imposing zero

---

[*] The consistent estimate of (Ω/N) is given by:

$$(\tilde{\Omega}/N)_{rs} = \sum_{i=1}^{N}(\tilde{v}_{ir}\tilde{v}_{is}Z_{ir}'Z_{is})/N,$$

where Z_{is} (t=r,s) is the ith row of Z_t and $\tilde{v}_{it}$ is the ith element of $\tilde{V}_t$. $\tilde{V}_t$ is the residual of the two stage least square(2SLS) regression for equation (A1). $\tilde{V}_t$ is calculated by:

$$\tilde{V}_t = Y_t - W_t\tilde{B}_t ,\ \text{where}\ \tilde{B}_t = [W_t'Z_t(Z_t'Z_t)^{-1}Z_t'W_t]^{-1}W_t'Z_t(Z_t'Z_t)^{-1}Z_t'Y_t .$$

constraints on the coefficients of the autoregressive system. For these problems, our test strategy is pretty similar to that of the Chow-type test. We first estimate the unrestricted and the restricted model and then calculate and compare the difference in the sum of square of residuals. We denote

$$Q = (Y-W\hat{B})'Z(\tilde{\Omega})^{-1}Z'\,(Y-W\hat{B})\,/\,N \qquad (A4)$$

which is the generalized sum of square of residuals of the system (A2). We calculate $L = Q_R - Q_U$, where Q_R and Q_U are respectively the generalized sum of square of residuals of the restricted and unrestricted systems, and use the following hypothesis testing procedure: If $L > L_\alpha$, we reject H_0. L follows a χ^2 distribution with degrees of freedom equal to the difference between the number of coefficients to be estimated in the two systems.[**] To calculate the Wald statistic, we note that :

$$\Theta = \text{Var}(\,\hat{B}) = [W'Z(\tilde{\Omega})^{-1}Z'W]^{-1} \qquad (A5)$$

[**] See H, N & R for the derivation of these statistics and their asymptotic distribution.

Appendix II

To get rid of β_i in equation (25) when there are more than one common risk factors in the market, we take equation (25) from period t to t-K+1 and "stack" them together as:

$$T_t \, \beta_i = \Phi_{it} \, .$$

where: $T_t{}' = [-\rho^{-1}(q_{t-1} - \rho m_t + n_t), ..., -\rho^{-1}(q_{t-K} - \rho m_{t-k+1} + n_{t-k+1})]$ and $\Phi_{it}{}' = [\, \delta_{i,t} - \rho^{-1}\delta_{i,t-1} - \rho^{-1}\Delta d_{i,t-1} + \rho^{-1}(r_{t-1} - \kappa') - (u_{i,t} - \rho^{-1}v_{i,t}), \, ... \, , \delta_{i,t-K+1} - \rho^{-1}\delta_{i,t-K} - \rho^{-1}\Delta d_{i,t-K} + \rho^{-1}(r_{t-K} - \kappa') - (u_{i,t-K+1} - \rho^{-1}v_{i,t-K+1})]$. T_t is a KxK matrix and Φ_{it} is a Kx1 vector.

We assume $T_t{}^{-1}$ exists, and solve for β_i:

$$\beta_i = T_t{}^{-1}\Phi_{it}.$$

Substituting it into equation (25) for period t+1, and denote:

$$G_t = (g_{1t}, ..., g_{Kt}) = \rho^{-1}(q_t - \rho m_{t+1} + n_{t+1})' \, T_t{}^{-1},$$

we obtain: $\quad \delta_{i,t+1} = -\rho^{-1}(r_t - \kappa') + \rho^{-1}\delta_{i,t} + \rho^{-1}\Delta d_{i,t} - G_t\Phi_{it} + u_{i,t+1} - \rho^{-1}v_{i,t+1}.$

Collecting terms, we have equation (29):

$$\delta_{i,t+1} = e_t + \sum_{J=0}^{K-1}\{(\rho^{-1}g_{Jt} - g_{J+1,t})\delta_{i,t-J} + \rho^{-1}g_{Jt}\Delta d_{i,t-J}\}$$

$$+ \rho^{-1}g_{Kt}\delta_{i,t-K} + \rho^{-1}g_{Kt}\Delta d_{i,t-K} + \mu_{i,t+1}, \qquad (29)$$

where:

$$e_t = -\rho^{-1}(r_t - \kappa') - \rho^{-1} \sum_{J=0}^{K} g_{Jt}(r_{t-J} - \kappa') \ ,$$

$$\mu_{i,t+1} = u_{i,t+1} - \rho^{-1} v_{i,t+1} + \sum_{J=0}^{K} g_{Jt}(u_{i,t-J+1} - \rho^{-1} v_{i,t-J+1}).$$

Table 1. Description of Data

===

Source: Expanded Compustat Annual Industrial File
       Standard & Poor's Compustat Service, Inc.

Selection Criteria: S & P 400 industrial companies continually listed on major
                   exchanges from 1969 to 1988 and always paying positive
                   annual dividends.

Number of securities
       selected: 257

Time period covered
       by the panel: 1969 to 1987

Variables selected   a) Previous year end closing price, $P_{i,t}$,
       from the file: b) Dividend paid during the year, $D_{i,t}$.

Variables constructed: a) log dividend-price ratio $\delta_{i,t}$
                         b) log dividend growth, $\Delta d_{i,t}$
                         c) log annual return, $h_{i,t}$
                         d) approximate log annual return, $\xi_{i,t}$.

===

Note: $\delta_{i,t}$, $\Delta d_{i,t}$, $h_{i,t}$ and $\xi_{i,t}$ are calculated as follows:

$$\delta_{i,t} = \log(D_{i,t-1}) - \log(P_{i,t}); \quad \Delta d_{i,t} = \log(D_{i,t}) - \log(D_{i,t-1})$$

$$h_{i,t} = \log(P_{i,t+1} + D_{i,t}) - \log(P_{i,t});$$

$$\xi_{i,t} = \kappa' + \rho \log(P_{i,t+1}) + (1-\rho)\log(D_{i,t}) - \log(P_{i,t});$$

where $\rho = \exp(\mathbf{g}\text{-}\mathbf{h})$, $\mathbf{g}$ is the mean annual log dividend growth , and $\mathbf{h}$ is the mean annual log return, $\kappa' = - \log(\rho) - (1- \rho)\log(1/\rho - 1)$.

Table 2. Summary Statistics for the Panel Data Set

A. Sample Means(Cross-section) for Each Year(1970-1987)

Year	70	71	72	73	74	75	76	77	78
$\delta_{i,t}$	-3.715	-3.886	-3.982	-3.625	-3.169	-3.462	-3.553	-3.294	-3.186
$\Delta d_{i,t}$	0.025	0.014	0.016	0.075	0.124	0.075	0.123	0.184	0.152
$h_{i,t}$	-0.002	0.210	0.135	-0.247	-0.281	0.405	0.245	-0.034	0.088
$\xi_{i,t}$	-0.007	0.205	0.129	-0.257	-0.294	0.399	0.241	-0.041	0.081

Year	79	80	81	82	83	84	85	86	87
$\delta_{i,t}$	-3.197	-3.239	-3.127	-3.290	-3.472	-3.385	-3.551	-3.364	-3.541
$\Delta d_{i,t}$	0.156	0.125	0.086	0.047	0.015	0.060	0.067	0.053	0.103
$h_{i,t}$	0.212	0.210	0.022	0.251	0.233	0.009	0.265	0.166	0.053
$\xi_{i,t}$	0.204	0.203	0.014	0.244	0.229	0.005	0.261	0.163	0.036

B. Grand(panel) Means

Var.	$\delta_{i,t}$	$\Delta d_{i,t}$	$h_{i,t}$	$\xi_{i,t}$
Mean	-3.4619	0.0834	0.1080	0.1008
Stan. Dev.	0.6773	0.2078	0.3062	0.3085

C. Estimated ρ (using equation given in Table I)
for calculating $\xi_{i,t}$ 0.9757

D. Correlation Coefficients between $h_{i,t}$ and $\xi_{i,t}$ 0.9944

Table 3. Test of Lag Length and Granger Causality for equation (16)
($\delta_{i,t}$ being $\zeta_{i,t}$)

$$h_{i,t} = \psi_{0t} + \sum_{J=1}^{K} \psi_{Jt} h_{i,t-J} + \pi_t \zeta_{i,t} + \eta_{i,t} \qquad (16)$$

A. Test of Lag Length K

==

Total lags K	Q	L	DF	P
(1) K=6	15.136	_	15	0.441
(2) K=5	24.486	9.350	5	0.095
(3) K=4	31.293	6.807	5	0.235
(4) K=3	40.303	9.010	5	0.108
(5) K=2	53.057	12.754	5	0.025

B. Test of non-Granger Causality($H_0 : \pi_t = 0$)

==

Total lags	Q	L	DF	P
(1) K=2 ($\pi_t = 0$)	75.700	22.643	5	0.000
(2) K=3 ($\pi_t = 0$)	48.451	8.238	5	0.143
(3) K=4 ($\pi_t = 0$)	39.619	8.326	5	0.139
(4) K=5 ($\pi_t = 0$)	37.058	12.572	5	0.027
(5) K=6 ($\pi_t = 0$)	20.124	4.988	5	0.417

Note: Returns from lag 7 to lag 13 and dividend-price ratios from lag 7 to lag 9 have been used as instruments. P gives the corresponding chi-square probability under which level the H_0 can be rejected.

Table 4. Estimates of Equation(16)(K=3)

$$h_{i,t} = \psi_{0t} + \sum_{J=1}^{K} \psi_{Jt} \, h_{i,t-J} + \pi_t \, \zeta_{i,t} + \eta_{i,t} \qquad (16)$$

Dep.var	cons.	$h_{i,t-1}$	$h_{i,t-2}$	$h_{i,t-3}$	$\delta_{i,t}$
Year=1983					
$h_{i,t}$	0.455*	-0.077	0.325	0.285	0.084
	(2.379)	(-0.261)	(0.773)	(0.818)	(1.584)
Year=1984					
$h_{i,t}$	0.562**	-0.600**	-0.165	0.533*	0.112*
	(3.114)	(-3.290)	(-0.976)	(2.769)	(2.349)
Year=1985					
$h_{i,t}$	0.051	0.644	0.220	0.186	-0.038
	(0.144)	(1.782)	(0.627)	(1.124)	(-0.399)
Year=1986					
$h_{i,t}$	0.423	1.056*	-0.567	-0.429	0.124
	(1.353)	(2.332)	(-1.358)	(-1.675)	(1.430)
Year=1987					
$h_{i,t}$	-0.157	1.677**	-1.879*	0.249	-0.118
	(-0.487)	(3.794)	(-2.129)	(0.333)	(-1.156)

Note: t-statistics is given in parentheses. We also report those t-values which exceed 2 by indicating them with one asterisk(*) and which exceed 3 by two asterisk(**). Returns from lag 7 to lag 13 and dividend-price ratios from lag 7 to lag 9 have been used as instruments.

Table 5. Test of Lag Length and Granger Causality for equation (16)
($\xi_{i,t}$ replacing $h_{i,t}$, $\delta_{i,t}$ being $\zeta_{i,t}$)

$$h_{i,t} = \psi_{0t} + \sum_{J=1}^{K} \psi_{Jt}\, h_{i,t-J} + \pi_t\, \zeta_{i,t} + \eta_{i,t} \qquad (16)$$

A.　Test of Lag Length K

Total lags K	L	DF	P
(1) K=6	–	–	–
(2) K=5	10.303	5	0.067
(3) K=4	7.832	5	0.165
(4) K=3	8.060	5	0.152
(5) K=2	15.111	5	0.009

B. Test of non-Granger Causality($H_0 : \pi_t = 0$)

Total lags	L	DF	P
(1) K=2 ($\pi_t = 0$)	22.495	5	0.000
(2) K=3 ($\pi_t = 0$)	8.647	5	0.123
(3) K=4 ($\pi_t = 0$)	9.219	5	0.100
(4) K=5 ($\pi_t = 0$)	13.533	5	0.018
(5) K=6 ($\pi_t = 0$)	5.424	5	0.366

Note: Returns from lag 7 to lag 13 and dividend-price ratios from lag 7 to lag 9 have been used as instruments. P gives the corresponding chi-square probability under which level the H_0 can be rejected.

Table 6. Test of Lag Length and Granger Causality for equation (16)
($\Delta d_{i,t}$ being $\zeta_{i,t}$)

$$h_{i,t} = \psi_{0t} + \sum_{J=1}^{K} \psi_{Jt} \, h_{i,t-J} + \pi_t \, \zeta_{i,t} + \eta_{i,t} \qquad\qquad (16)$$

A. Test of Lag Length K

Total lags K	L	DF	P
(1) K=6	–	–	–
(2) K=5	6.270	5	0.280
(3) K=4	1.989	5	0.850
(4) K=3	14.506	5	0.012
(5) K=2	14.138	5	0.011

B. Test of non-Granger Causality($H_0 : \pi_t = 0$)

Total lags	L	DF	P
(1) K=2 ($\pi_t = 0$)	4.988	5	0.417
(2) K=3 ($\pi_t = 0$)	8.451	5	0.133
(3) K=4 ($\pi_t = 0$)	11.081	5	0.049
(4) K=5 ($\pi_t = 0$)	9.871	5	0.078
(5) K=6 ($\pi_t = 0$)	6.960	5	0.223

Note: Returns from lag 7 to lag 13 and dividend growth from lag 7 to lag 9 have been used as instruments. P gives the corresponding chi-square probability under which level the H_0 can be rejected.

Table 7. Test of non-Granger Causality for equation (20)(Ho: $\gamma_{Jt} = 0$)

$$\delta_{i,t} = \beta_{0t} + \sum_{J=1}^{p+K} \beta_{Jt}\delta_{i,t-J} + \sum_{J=1}^{p+K} \gamma_{Jt}\Delta d_{i,t-J-1} + \varpi_{i,t} \qquad (20)$$

Total lags m=p+K	L	DF	P
(1) m=3	37.938	15	0.0009
(2) m=4	35.518	20	0.0175
(3) m=5	28.073	25	0.3045
(4) m=6	28.489	30	0.5445

Note: $\delta_{i,t}$ and $\Delta d_{i,t-1}$ from lag 7 to lag 13 have been used as instruments. P gives the corresponding chi-square probability under which level the Ho can be rejected.

*   *   *

Table 8. Test of non-Granger Causality for equation (21) (Ho: $\phi_{Jt} = 0$)

$$\Delta d_{i,t-1} = \phi_{0t} + \sum_{J=1}^{p+K} \phi_{Jt}\delta_{i,t-J} + \sum_{J=1}^{p+K} \lambda_{Jt}\Delta d_{i,t-J-1} + \upsilon_{i,t} \qquad (21)$$

Total lags m=p+K	L	DF	P
(1) m=3	48.207	15	0.0000
(2) m=4	28.934	20	0.0891
(3) m=5	29.818	25	0.2311
(4) m=6	30.706	30	0.4272

Note: $\delta_{i,t}$ and $\Delta d_{i,t-1}$ from lag 7 to lag 13 have been used as instruments. P gives the corresponding chi-square probability under which level the Ho can be rejected.

Table 9. VAR with Time-varying Coefficients (m=p+K=3)

$$\delta_{i,t} = \beta_{0t} + \sum_{J=1}^{p+K} \beta_{Jt}\delta_{i,t-J} + \sum_{J=1}^{p+K} \gamma_{Jt}\Delta d_{i,t-J-1} + \varpi_{i,t} \qquad (20)$$

$$\Delta d_{i,t-1} = \phi_{0t} + \sum_{J=1}^{p+K} \phi_{Jt}\delta_{i,t-J} + \sum_{J=1}^{p+K} \lambda_{Jt}\Delta d_{i,t-J-1} + \upsilon_{i,t} \qquad (21)$$

Dep.var	cons.	$\delta_{i,t-1}$	$\Delta d_{i,t-2}$	$\delta_{i,t-2}$	$\Delta d_{i,t-3}$	$\delta_{i,t-3}$	$\Delta d_{i,t-4}$
Year = 1983							
$\delta_{i,t-1}$	-0.382	0.942**	0.864	-0.148	-2.430*	0.143	1.343
	(-0.906)	(3.839)	(1.407)	(-0.239)	(-2.326)	(0.369)	(1.371)
$\Delta d_{i,t-2}$	0.341	-0.128**	1.253	0.082	-2.078*	0.179	1.661**
	(0.906)	(3.839)	(1.407)	(-0.239)	(-2.326)	(0.369)	(1.371)
Year=1984							
$\delta_{i,t-1}$	-0.742*	0.167	1.087	0.924*	-0.543	-0.324	-0.228
	(-2.891)	(0.472)	(1.585)	(2.043)	(-1.559)	(-1.833)	(-0.655)
$\Delta d_{i,t-2}$	0.052	-0.112	0.684	0.183	-0.109	-0.077	-0.138
	(0.204)	(-0.427)	(1.229)	(0.620)	(-0.368)	(-0.737)	(-0.584)
Year=1985							
$\delta_{i,t-1}$	0.146	1.477**	-0.140	0.278	-0.628	-0.706*	-0.379
	(0.524)	(3.393)	(-0.274)	(0.545)	(-1.403)	(-2.654)	(-1.061)
$\Delta d_{i,t-2}$	-0.074	-0.266	0.205	0.156	0.394**	0.065	0.044
	(-0.609)	(-1.696)	(1.272)	(0.965)	(3.008)	(0.956)	(0.655)

Table 9. VAR with Time-varying Coefficients (m=p+K=3) (Continued)

Dep.var	cons.	$\delta_{i,t-1}$	$\Delta d_{i,t-2}$	$\delta_{i,t-2}$	$\Delta d_{i,t-3}$	$\delta_{i,t-3}$	$\Delta d_{i,t-4}$
Year = 1986							
$\delta_{i,t-1}$	-0.723	1.837**	-1.446	-2.335**	0.700	1.222*	-0.188
	(-2.310)	(5.500)	(-1.510)	(-3.198)	(1.361)	(2.725)	(-0.625)
$\Delta d_{i,t-2}$	-0.224	-0.221	-1.867*	0.401	-0.269	0.502	0.766*
	(-0.714)	(1.324)	(-2.852)	(-0.711)	(-0.585)	(1.221)	(2.546)
Year=1987							
$\delta_{i,t-1}$	-0.704	0.847	-0.842	-0.306	1.749	0.255	-1.201
	(-0.885)	(0.958)	(-0.759)	(-0.267)	(1.353)	(0.430)	(-0.792)
$\Delta d_{i,t-2}$	-0.985*	-0.921	0.484	0.985	0.480	-0.387	-2.030*
	(-2.004)	(-1.289)	(0.414)	(0.708)	(0.374)	(-0.486)	(-2.123)

Note: t-statistics is given in parenthese. We also report those t-values which exceed 2 by indicating them with one asterisk(*) and which exceed 3 by two asterisks(**).

Table 10. Comparison with Campbell and Shiller's Estimates

A) Campbell and Shiller's VAR model with constant coefficients(p=1) and
   real discount rate based on Cowles/S & P 500 (1871-1986)

Dep.var	$\delta_{i,t-1}$	$\Delta d_{i,t-2}$	Joint significance of coeff.
$\delta_{i,t}$	0.706 (0.066)	0.259 (0.139)	0.000
$\Delta d_{i,t-1}$	-0.197 (0.039)	0.231 (0.083)	0.000

B) Corresponding VAR model with constant coefficients(p=1) and 257
   S & P 400 industrials companies (1982-1987)

Dep.var	Cons.	$\delta_{i,t-1}$	$\Delta d_{i,t-2}$	Joint significance of coeff.
$\delta_{i,t}$	-0.717 (0.085)	0.798 (0.025)	-0.846 (0.094)	0.000
$\Delta d_{i,t-1}$	-0.261 (0.036)	-0.096 (0.010)	0.019 (0.029)	0.000

Table 11. Test Equation(30) (K=2)

$$\delta_{i,t+1} = f_t + \sum_{J=0}^{K} \{ \eta_{Jt}\delta_{i,t-J} + \theta_{Jt}\Delta d_{i,t-J} \} + \mu_{i,t+1} \qquad (30)$$

Dep.var		cons.	$\Delta d_{i,t}$	$\delta_{i,t}$	$\Delta d_{i,t-1}$	$\delta_{i,t-1}$	$\Delta d_{i,t-2}$	$\delta_{i,t-2}$
1983	$\delta_{i,t+1}$	-0.451	1.067*	0.831**	0.609	0.550	-0.604	-0.437
		(-1.983)	(2.153)	(3.109)	(1.029)	(0.934)	(-0.751)	(-1.278)
1984	$\delta_{i,t+1}$	-0.309	1.353*	0.508	0.805	0.766*	-0.918*	-0.372*
		(-1.394)	(2.798)	(1.805)	(1.450)	(2.095)	(-2.300)	(-2.232)
1985	$\delta_{i,t+1}$	0.267	1.198	2.370**	-1.585*	-0.872	-0.844	-0.358
		(0.650)	(1.193)	(4.208)	(-2.322)	(-1.264)	(-1.007)	(-0.847)
1986	$\delta_{i,t+1}$	-0.642	0.295	1.981**	-1.565	-2.613**	0.934	1.374*
		(-1.814)	(0.548)	(6.329)	(-1.850)	(-3.630)	(1.685)	(2.884)
1987	$\delta_{i,t+1}$	0.002	0.494	1.435*	-0.028	-0.697	1.593	0.291
		(0.005)	(1.264)	(2.059)	(-0.026)	(-0.563)	(1.450)	(0.436)

Note: t-statistics is given in parentheses. We also report those t-values which exceed 2 by indicating them with one asterisk(*) and which exceed 3 by two asterisks(**).

Table 12. Wald Test of Hypothesis (31)

$$\delta_{i,t+1}= f_t +\sum_{J=0}^{K}\{\,\eta_{Jt}\delta_{i,t-J}+\theta_{Jt}\Delta d_{i,t-J}\} + \mu_{i,t+1} \qquad (30)$$

$$H_0:\ \eta_{Kt}=\theta_{Kt}\,,\,(\,\theta_{Jt}-\eta_{Jt})\,\theta_{0t}-\theta_{J+1,t}=0 \qquad (J=0\!\sim\!K\text{-}1). \qquad (31)$$

K	Year	1983	1984	1985	1986	1987	Joint test
K=5	Wald-S.	2.817	5.621	0.870	1.001	4.534	19.541
DF=6	P	0.831	0.466	0.990	0.985	0.604	0.927
K=4	Wald-S.	2.162	2.639	1.688	2.578	3.169	17.835
DF=5	P	0.826	0.755	0.890	0.764	0.673	0.849
K=3	Wald-S.	5.816	3.332	1.114	4.532	2.919	33.350
DF=4	P	0.213	0.505	0.982	0.338	0.571	0.031*
K=2	Wald-S.	7.108	5.877	2.155	2.199	2.260	42.825
DF=3	P	0.069*	0.117	0.540	0.532	0.520	0.021*

Note: The degrees of freedom(DF) of each year's Wald test are the same as the number of total lags m. While the DF for joint test is 5(K+1). The first row gives the nonlinear Wald-statistics, the second row gives the significance levels under the Ho. Asterisk(*) indicates rejection of the hypothesis.

Application of the Newey-West Matrix for Correction of Heteroskedasticity and Cross-Sectional Correlation

Jianping Mei

&

Whitney Newey*

Department of Economics
Princeton University
Princeton, New Jersey 08544

* We would like to thank David Card and Bob Korajczyk for very helpful discussion. We are also grateful to Gordon Bodnar, Stephen Brown, Gregory Chow, Angus Deaton, David Genesove for helpful comments. We thank them without implications.

I. Introduction

Although the Newey-West (1987) adjustment is now a standard procedure used by econometrician to correct for heteroskedasticity and autocorrelation in time series models, few seems to have realized its applicability for correction of cross- sectional correlation and heteroskedasticity in panel study.

In many previous empirical work, it is generally assumed that there exist no cross-sectional correlation across firms, such as Brown and Warner (1980), (1985), Christie (1985), Holtz-Eakin, Newey and Rosen (1988) and Mei (1989). Although this assumption might be a fairly good approximation in some cases, it is certainly restrictive and can not be applied to general situations. It is conceivable that, in the arbitrage pricing model studied by Mei (1989), there exist industry effects that are not pervasive economic factors but nonetheless introduce cross-sectional correlation into the linear factor model that will violate the above no correlation assumption. Failure to account for the contemporaneous correlation often leads to biased estimates of standard errors of parameters and unreliable inference, as pointed out by Deaton and Irish (1983).

In a recent paper by Kenneth Froot, he argues that standard correction procedures for entire cross section, such as GLS, are often difficult to implement in practice because the panel data used in many accounting and finance study has a large number of firms but relatively few time series observations. Thus, he proposes a method-of-moments technique which is similar to that of Hansen (1982) and further suggests the use of a two-stage-least-square estimation procedure of Cragg (1983) to improve asymptotic efficiency.

Unfortunately, the linear regression model studied by Froot seems to be too simple and restrictive to be of wide applicability. Drawing on the analogies with the problem of serial correlation and heteroskedasticity in time series study, where the Newey-West heteroskedasticity and autocorrelation consistent matrix is used for correction, this paper shows that the Newey-West procedure is applicable to a more general nonlinear model for panel data as long as some regulatory conditions spelled out in the appendix are satisfied. The procedure allows for intertemporal correlation between error terms and regressors of different times. It relaxes the assumption of constant parameters over time and replaces the block diagonal error structure by a mixing condition as defined by White (1984).

The paper will be organized as follows: Section II presents the modified Newey-West heteroskedasticity and cross-section correlation consistent covariance matrix with an application to a problem of estimating vector autoregressions with panel data. Section III applies the method to an example from finance; which investigates the number of pervasive economic factors in the financial markets. Section IV concludes.

II. The Modified Newey-West Covariance Matrix

In the usual cross-section or panel study context, estimating θ using the orthogonality condition $Eh(Z_i, \theta^*) = 0$ typically involve the solution to the following problem:

$$\text{Min}_\theta \; h_N(\theta)'(S_N)^{-1} h_N(\theta). \tag{1}$$

where $h_N(\theta) = \sum_{i=1}^{N} h(Z_i, \theta^*)/N$ is the vector of sample monents of $h(Z_i, \theta^*)$ and S_N is a symmetric weighting matrix. Here N is the number of cross-sectional observations. Assuming the data Z_i and the functional form of $h(Z_i, \theta^*)$ satisfy the regulatory conditions of White and Domowitz (1984), then, the asymptotic covariance matrix of the optimal GMM estimator θ is given by

$$V_N = (H_N'(S_N)^{-1} H_N)^{-1}.$$

where $H_N = \sum_{i=1}^{N} E[h_{i\theta}(\theta^*)]/N$ and $h_{i\theta}(\theta^*)$ is the (rxk) matrix of partial derivative of $h_i(\theta^*)$. And S_N is defined as $\sum_{j=1}^{N} \sum_{i=1}^{N} E[h_i(\theta^*)h_i(\theta^*)']/N$. S_N is unknown and must be estimated.

Parallel to the time series case studied by Newey and West, if the data satisfy some similar regulatory conditions given in the appendix, then a consistent estimator of S_N can be derived from the Newey-West covariance matrix by simply replacing the time index with a cross-section index i. Thus, it will take the form:

$$\widehat{S}_N = \widehat{\Omega}_0 + \sum_{j=1}^{M} w(j,M)[\widehat{\Omega}_j + \widehat{\Omega}_j'], \quad \widehat{\Omega}_j = \sum_{i=j+1}^{N} h_i(\widehat{\theta})h_{i-j}(\widehat{\theta})'/N, \quad w(j,M) = 1- [j/(M+1)]. \tag{3}$$

Here, $\hat{\theta}$ is some preliminary consistent estimates of θ. The bound M puts a limit on how much cross-sectional correlation that are allowed to have among different individuals. It implicitly assumes that under some proper ordering (or indexing) of the sample, The dependence between $h_i(\theta)$ and $h_j(\theta)$ that are far apart, meaning $|i-j| > M$, is negligible by the mixing condition. Note, although M is a fixed number in a finite sample, it can grow with the sample size as long as it grows at a slower rate.

Unlike time series data, where there is a natural ordering of sample by time, and the condition of negligible dependence between $h_t(\theta)$ and $h_s(\theta)$, for $|t-s| > M$, holds naturally in many cases, it is generally quite difficult to find an appropriate ordering of cross-sectional data such that similar condition holds. Only for some special cases, the econometricain may be able to get some clues from economic theory. For example, in the Arbitrage Pricing Theory studied by Mei (1989), it is quite reasonable to assume that the idiosyncratic shocks of firms within a same industry are correlated but the shocks of firms of different industry are not correlated. Thus, if we sort the data by industry and let M be the number of firms in the largest industry, then if $|i-j| > M$, we will have negligible dependence between $h_i(\theta)$ and $h_j(\theta)$, for firm i and j will certainly come from different industries.

A Special Case

An interesting application of the above result is to allow for some cross-sectional correlation in the vector autoregression model studied by Holtz-Eakin, Newey and Rosen (1989) (HNR), using panel data. Their model takes the following form after pseudo-differencing:

$$y_{it} = a_t + \sum_{q=1}^{k} c_{qt} y_{i,t-q} + \sum_{q=1}^{k} d_{qt} x_{i,t-q} + v_{it}. \qquad i=1,...,N. \quad t=k+1,...,T. \qquad (4)$$

where the data satisfy the following orthoganality conditions:

$$E(y_{is}v_{it}) = E(x_{is}v_{it}) = 0. \qquad (s < t-1) \qquad (5)$$

Here, we relax the no cross-sectional correlation assumption made by HNR. Instead, we assume $\{ v_{it}, i=1,...,\infty \}$ is a α-mixing process.

It is easy to see that this model is not a special case of the Froot model, because it allows intertemporal dependence among v_{it} and the autoregressors. The parameters are time varying and the autoregressors are correlated with the error terms.

Following HNR's notation, we write:

$$Y_t = (y_{1,t}, y_{2,t}, ... y_{N,t})' \qquad\qquad X_t = (x_{1,t}, x_{2,t}, ..., x_{N,t})'$$

as Nx1 vectors of observations for a given time period t . Let

$$W_t = (e, Y_{t-1}, ..., Y_{t-k}, X_{t-1}, ..., X_{t-k})$$

be Nx(2k+1) Matrix of the right-hand side (RHS) variables of (4). e is a Nx1 vector of ones. Denote V_t be the vector of the error terms, and let $B_t = (a_t, c_{1t}, ... c_{Kt}, d_{1t}, ..., d_{Kt})'$. Then equation (4) can be written as:

$$Y_t = W_t B_t + V_t . \qquad\qquad t = K+1, ..., T . \qquad\qquad (6)$$

To combine equation (6) over time into system of equations, we "stack" equation (6) by time:

$$\begin{bmatrix} Y_{K+1} \\ \vdots \\ Y_T \end{bmatrix} = \begin{bmatrix} W_{K+1} & \cdots & 0 \\ \vdots & \ddots & \vdots \\ 0 & \cdots & W_T \end{bmatrix} \begin{bmatrix} B_{K+1} \\ \vdots \\ B_T \end{bmatrix} + \begin{bmatrix} V_{K+1} \\ \vdots \\ V_T \end{bmatrix}, \qquad (7)$$

Thus, equation (7) can be written as :

$$Y = WB + V . \qquad\qquad (8)$$

If we denote $Z_t = (e, Y_{t-2}, ..., Y_1, X_{t-2}, ..., X_1)$ and let Z_{it} be i-th row of Z_t, we can rewrite the orthoganality condition (5) as

$$E(Z_{it}'v_{it}) = 0. \qquad\qquad t = k+1, ..., T. \qquad\qquad (9)$$

Denoting $h(Z_i, B) = (v_{i,k+1} Z_{i,k+1}, ..., v_{iT} Z_{iT})'$, we choose B^* as the optimal GMM estimator which is the solution to:

$$Min_B \ h_N(B)'(S_N)^{-1} h_N(B). \qquad\qquad (10)$$

where $h_N = Z'V/N = \sum_{i=1}^{N} h(z_i,B)/N$ and $S_N = E(Z'VV'Z)/N = E(\sum_{i=1}^{N} \sum_{j=1}^{N} h(z_i,B)h(z_j,B)'/N)$.

Since $h(Z_i,B)$ is linear in B, it is easily shown that the above GMM estimator is the same as an instrumental variable estimator obtained from applying generalized least squares (GLS) to the following equation[1]:

$$Z'Y = Z'WB + Z'V. \qquad (11)$$

where the covariance matrix of the transformed error terms, Z'V, is given by

$$\Pi = NS_N = E(Z'VV'Z). \qquad (12)$$

If Π were known, the GLS estimator of B would be:

$$B^* = [W'Z(\Pi)^{-1}Z'W]^{-1}W'Z(\Pi)^{-1}Z'Y \qquad (13)$$

Since Π is not known, we need to find a consistent estimate for it. According to our previous discussion, we can certainly use the modified Newey-West matrix, if we can find a preliminary consistent estimate of B. If we let $\tilde{B}$ be such an estimate and $\hat{V}_t = Y_t - W_t \tilde{B}_t$, then use equation (3), we have:

$$(\hat{S}_N)_{rs} = \hat{\Omega}_0 + \sum_{j=1}^{M} w(j,M)[\hat{\Omega}_j + \hat{\Omega}_j'], \ \hat{\Omega}_j = \sum_{i=j+1}^{N} v_{ir}v_{i-j,s}Z_{ir}Z_{i-j,s}', \ w(j,M)=1-[j/(M+1)]. \ (14)$$

where v_{ir} is the i th element of $\hat{V}_t$ and Z_{ir} is the i th row of Z_t.

Using $\Pi = NS_N$ and replacing Π with $\hat{\Pi}$ in (13), we get:

$$\hat{B} = \{W'Z(\hat{\Pi})^{-1}Z'W\}^{-1} W'Z(\hat{\Pi})^{-1}Z'Y. \qquad (15)$$

The estimates is consistent despite the existence of cross sectional correlation and heteroskedasticity over time and across securities. In order to test some linear restrictions imposed on the estimated parameters, we consider the

---

[1] Note, here the GLS is applies to the tranformed error term, Z'V , to minimize $V'Z \Pi^{-1} Z'V$, instead of the error term of the entire cross-section, V, to minimize $V' \Omega^{-1} V$. The later is difficult to implement as pointed out by Froot.

following null hypothesis:

$$H_0: \quad B = H\gamma + G. \tag{16}$$

where γ is a px1 vector of parameters, H is a constant matrix and G is a constant vector. If we denote Q being the unrestricted sum of squared residuals and Q_R being the restricted sum of squared residuals, i.e.,

$$Q = (Y-W\hat{B})'Z(\hat{\Pi})^{-1}Z'(Y-W\hat{B})/N, \quad Q_R = (Y-\widetilde{W}\hat{\gamma})'Z(\hat{\Pi})^{-1}Z'(Y-\widetilde{W}\hat{\gamma})/N. \tag{17}$$

It is shown by HNR that the difference in the sum of squared residuals, L ($L = Q_R - Q$), will have an asymptotic χ^2 distribution with degrees of freedom equal to the difference between the number of parameters to be estimated in both cases. See HNR for details.

III. An Example

In this section, we will develop a χ^2 test statistic to determine the number of factors in an approximate factor model of asset returns.

1) The Model

Assume returns on assets are generated by the following K-factor model:

$$R_{it} = \alpha_{i,t} + f_{1t}\beta_{i1} + ... + f_{Kt}\beta_{iK} + \varepsilon_{it} \qquad i = 1,...,N; \qquad t = 1,...,T. \tag{18}$$

where

$\alpha_{i,t}$ is the expected return on asset i conditional on information set I_t known at the beginning of period t.

$f_t' = (f_{1t},...,f_{Kt})$ is a vector of unobservable random factors with time-varying distributions;

$(\beta_{i1},..., \beta_{iK})$ is a vector of factor loadings which are time invariant; and

ε_{it} represents an idiosyncratic risk specific to asset i;

We assume that { ε_{it}, t=1,...,T} is a series of independently distributed random vectors with

$$E(\varepsilon_t) = 0; \quad E(f_t) = 0; \quad Cov(f_t, f_t) = \Lambda_t; \quad E(\varepsilon_t | f_t) = 0; \quad E(\varepsilon_t \varepsilon_t' | f_t) = D_t.$$

where Λ_t is diagonal. We assume f_t are independent over time.

Unlike the strict factor model studied by Ross (1976), which assumes D_t being diagonal, we assume the cross-sectional sequence { ε_{it}, i=1,...,∞} is a α-mixing process. The mixing condition allows some off-diagonal elements of D_t to be nonzero, but it restricts the correlation of ε_{it} that are far apart to "die off" as they become further apart.

According to Connor and Korajczyk (1988b), the mixing condition implies an approximate factor structure that was studied by Chamberlain and Rothschild (1983) and Ingersoll (1984). This structure can be used to derive the following approximate linear pricing relationship:

$$\alpha_{i,t} = \lambda_{0t} + \lambda_{1t}\beta_{i1} +...+ \lambda_{Kt}\beta_{iK}, \tag{19}$$

where $(\lambda_{1t},..., \lambda_{Kt})$ is a vector of risk premia corresponding to
the risk factors $(f_{1t},...,f_{Kt})$; and
λ_{0t} is the return on a riskless (or "zero beta") asset.

Combining (18) and the linear pricing equation (19) and denoting $s_t' = (s_{1t},...,s_{Kt}) =(f_{1t},...,f_{Kt})+ (\lambda_{1t},..., \lambda_{Kt})$ and $\beta_i' = (\beta_{i1},..., \beta_{iK})$, we obtain,

$$R_{i,t} = \lambda_{0t} + s_t'\beta_i + \varepsilon_{i,t}. \qquad i=1,..., N; t=1,...,T. \tag{20}$$

To get rid of the unobservable β_i in (20), we take equation (20) for asset i from time period t-1 to t-K, and "stack" them on top of one another and move λ_{0t} and $\varepsilon_{i,t}$ to the other side, and denote :

$$S_t = \begin{bmatrix} s_{1,t-1} & \cdots & s_{K,t-1} \\ \vdots & \vdots & \vdots \\ s_{1,t-K} & \cdots & s_{K,t-K} \end{bmatrix} \qquad \Pi_t = \begin{bmatrix} R_{i,t-1}-\lambda_{0,t-1}-\varepsilon_{i,t-1} \\ \vdots \\ R_{i,t-K}-\lambda_{0,t-K}-\varepsilon_{i,t-K} \end{bmatrix}$$

S_t is a KxK matrix and Π_{it} is a Kx1 matrix. Thus, we have,

$$S_t \beta_i = \Pi_{it}.$$

Assume there are no redundant factors in the model so that S_t is non-singular. We solve for β_i, and substituting it into (20) for time period t, we have:

$$R_{i,t} = \lambda_{0t} + s_t' \, S_t^{-1} \, \Pi_{it} + \varepsilon_{i,t} \, . \qquad\qquad i=1,\dots,\; N,\; t=K+1,\dots,T.$$

Collecting terms, and defining $\psi_t' =(\psi_{1t},\dots,\psi_{Kt}) = s_t' \, S_t^{-1}$, we have,

$$R_{i,t} = \psi_{0t} + \sum_{j=1}^{K} \psi_{jt} \, R_{i,t-j} + \eta_{i,t} \, . \qquad i=1,\dots,N;\quad t=K+1,\dots,T. \qquad (21)$$

where:

$$\psi_{0,t} = \lambda_{0t} - \sum_{j=1}^{K} \psi_{jt}\, \lambda_{0,t-j} \qquad \eta_{i,t} = \varepsilon_{it} - \sum_{j=1}^{K} \psi_{jt}\, \varepsilon_{i,t-j}. \qquad t=K+1,\dots,T. \qquad (22)$$

Therefore, we have transformed the K-factor model of (18) into a K-lag autoregression model of (21). We can see that the autoregressors $R_{i,t-j}$ (j=1,\dots,K) are correlated with the error term η_{it} through their correlation with $\varepsilon_{it-1},\dots,\varepsilon_{it-K}$ and there is heteroskedasticity and serial correlation in the error term, η_{it}. It is also easy to see η_{it} has mean zero conditional on ψ_{jt}, which are functions of current and past f_t. We also have: $E(R_{i,t-s}\,\eta_{it}) = 0$ (s > K). Since $R_{i,t-s}$ (s > K) are correlated cross sectionally with $R_{i,t-s}$ (s < K) on the right hand side of (21), they can be used as instruments for estimating the parameters of (21). Other variables, which are known at time t-k and are correlated with the autoregressors, such as securities' prices and dividend yields, also qualify as potential instruments.

From the definition of mixing process, it is easy to see that { η_{it}, i=1,\dots,\infty} is α-mixing, given ψ_{jt} known and { ε_{it}, i=1,\dots,\infty} being α-mixing. This results was given by Lemma 2.1 of White and Domowitz (1984).

Thus, autoregression system (21) satisfy the conditions given in Section II, which can be estimated using a three-stage-least-square procedure. The parameter estimates will be consistent despite the existence of cross sectional correlation and heteroskedas- ticity over time and across securities.

Using the results we derived in Section II, we know the unrestricted sum of squared residuals, Q, will have a χ^2 distribution if the K factor model of (18) is correctly specified. In this case, if we impose the restriction that model (18) only has K-1 factors, i.e., autoregression (21) has K-1 lags, we must have a larger than usual restricted sum of squared residuals, Q_R, that will cause a rejection of the K-1 model through a χ^2 test, which takes the difference between Q and Q_R. The intuition is that if the Kth factor is pervasive, it will tend to cause a lot contemporaneous dependence among the shocks, ε_{it}, of the K-1 model and make them violate the mixing conditions. Under this circumstance, the adjustment for cross sectional correlations made by (14) will not be enough and the sum of squared residuals will tend to be bigger than it should be.

By the same token, if the model is correct, we should not be able to reject H_0: $\pi_t = 0$ in the following regression:

$$R_{i,t} = \psi_{0t} + \sum_{j=1}^{K} \psi_{jt} R_{i,t-j} + \pi_t C_{i,t-K} + \eta_{i,t} . \qquad i=1,...,N; \quad t=K+1,...,T. \qquad (23)$$

where C_{it} represents a firm specific variable such as log capitalization. The rejection of $\pi_t = 0$ indicates the existence of a size anomaly. The reason behind this is that firm size should not have any explanatory power over η_{it}, which is a linear combination of future random errors.

2. Data

The estimation and testing are conducted by a GAUSS program using an IBM PS/2. The securities selected into our panel data set are stocks contained in the December 1988 version of the CRSP monthly return file. The time period covered by the panel is 1987.1-1988.12. Securities with missing information on returns, prices and shares outstanding during the time period covered by the panel are excluded.

We sort the firms in the panel first by their 4-digit SIC industry code and within a industry we then sort the firms by their CUSIP numbers. We assume the cross-sectional correlations are mainly caused by industry effects. And there is no correlation of idiosyncratic shocks between firms of different industries. Since the largest industry has 88 firms, we set the M in equation (3) to be 88.

3. Estimation of Regression (21) and Test of Minimum Lag Length, K.

Using the data set constructed from the CRSP monthly return file, we estimate (21) for the last 6 months of 1988 and use the earlier 18 months data for lags and instruments.

Table 2a presents some test results of how many lags we should use in the autoregressions. The first column of Table 2a specifies the number of lag length, K, in the regression. The second column gives the generalized sum of squared residuals, Q, corresponding to each specification. The third column provides the difference in the generalized sum of squared residuals between its corresponding specification and the specification above it, which has one more lag. It measures the reduction in the generalized sum of squared residuals by the introduction of one more lag into the regression. For example, $L_{(K=8,2a)} = Q_{(K=8,2a)} - Q_{(K=9,2a)} = 18.455-18.203 = 0.252$. If the specification is true, we expect L to be small. Under the null hypothesis, L has a χ^2 distribution with degrees of freedom given by the fourth column. The last column gives the significance level by which the specification can be rejected.

We start by estimating (21) with K=9. As Table 2a show, we can not reject the hypothesis that equation (21) might have 7 lags for the last six month of 1988. For example, the L value for K=7 (0.388) in 2a tells us that we can not reject K=7 (P=0.998). But the specification of K=5,6 are strongly rejected (P=0.000), suggesting equation (21) needs at least 7 lags. This indicates there are at least 7 systematic factors at work in the market during this time period.

Table 3a presents a parallel study when we impose the restriction that there is no cross-sectional correlations across shocks ε_{it}. The test results suggest a 7 factor model be necessary, while indicating additional factors might help further reduce the generalized sum of squared residuals. This is exactly what we would expect. Because by imposing the restriction of the covariance matrix of ε_{it} being diagonal, we have to introduce more factors into the model to pick up those off-diagonal elements that are actually exist.

4. An Examination of the "Size Anomaly"

Table 2b presents the test results based on several specifications of K, since we can not tell exactly how many risk factors are in the market. The second column of Table 2b gives the generalized sum of squared residuals, Q, of regression (23). The third column gives the difference in the generalized sum of squared residuals of the restricted ($\pi_t = 0$) model, which is regression (21), and the unrestricted model. The generalized sum of squared residuals of the restricted model, Q, is given in Table 2a. Thus, we calculate $L_{(K=9,2b)} = Q_{(K=9,2a)} - Q_{(K=9,2b)} = 18.203-16.872 = 1.331$, etc.

From Table 2b, we can see that $\pi_t = 0$ is rejected for $K < 7$, but not for $K \geq 7$. So our interpretation is that the introduction of more risk factors into the APT model can capture the size effect found in models with less risk factors.

The test of "size anomaly" under no cross-sectional correlation gives similar results, which is given in table 3b.

Table 4 and 5 present the parameter estimates of (23) for both cases. We can see that the parameter estimates are quite close to each other, suggesting the robustness of the estimates. What is more interesting is that the t-statistics with Newey-West adjustment are generally larger than those without. This suggests the existence of considerable amount of cross-sectional correlation among the idiosyncratic shocks of firms studied so that correcting them actually improves the standard errors of the estimates. This result is similar to that of Froot, who found considerable efficiency gains by using the method of moments technique instead of OLS in his simulation study.

IV. Conclusion

We have shown that the Newey-West adjustment can be very useful for cross-sectional and panel study. We applied that adjustment procedure to the vector autoregression system by Holtz-Eakin, Newey and Rosen and developed a χ^2 test to determine the number of pervasive factors in an approximate factor model.

Our empirical results suggest there are seven factors at work in the economy from 1987 to 1988. Comparing with a pioneering study on the same subject by Connor and Korajczyk (1988b), our test procedure are not dependent on the use of long time series data to obtain a consistent estimate of the idiosyncratic shocks. But ours has the drawback of explicitly sorting the data in some ways and assuming the idiosyncratic shocks that are far apart by the sorting are not correlated. Like their test procedure, ours is also simple, intuitive and easy to implement.

104

References

Brown, S., and J. Warner, 1980, "Measuring Security Price Performance." Journal of Financial Economics, 8, 205-258.

Brown, S., and J. Warner, 1985, "Using Daily Stock Returns: The Case of Event Stuies." Journal of Financial Economics, 14, 3-35.

Brown, Stephen J. and Mark T. Weinstein, 1983, "A New Approach to Testing Arbitrage Pricing Models: The Bilinear Paradigm," Journal of Finance, 38, 711-743.

Brown, P., A. Kleidon and T. Marsh, 1983, "New Evidence on the nature of Size Related Anomalies in Stock Prices", Journal of Financial Economics, 12, 33-56.

Chamberlain, Gary, 1983, "Panel Data," Chapter 22 in the handbook of Econometrics Volume II, ed. by Z. Griliches and M. Intrilligator. Amsterdam: North-Holland Publishing Company.

Chen, Nai-fu, 1983, "Some Empirical Tests of the Theory of Arbitrage Pricing." Journal of Finance, 38, 1392-1414.

Chen, Nai-fu, Richard Roll and Stephen Ross, 1986, "Economic Forces and the Stock Market ." Journal of Business, 59, 386-403.

Cho, Chinhyung D., Edwin J. Elton and Martin J. Gruber, 1984,"On the Robustness of the Roll and Ross Arbitrage Pricing Theory", Journal of Financial and Quantitative Analysis, 19, 1-10.

Christie, A., 1985, "On Cross-Sectional Analysis in Acconting Research." Working Paper, University of Southern California.

Connor, Gregory and Robert A. Korajczyk, 1988a, "Risk and Return in an Equilibrium APT: Application of a New Test Methodology" Journal of Financial Economics, 21, 255-289.

Connor, Gregory and Robert A. Korajczyk, 1988b, "A Test for the Number of Factors in An Approximate Factor Model". Working Paper .

Cragg, John G., 1983,"More Efficient Estimation in the Presence of Hetroskedasticity of Unknown Form." Econometrica, 51, 751-763.

Froot, Kenneth, 1989, "Consistent Covariance Matrix Estimation with Cross-Sectional Dependence and Heteroskedasticity in Financial Data", Journal of Financial and Quantitative Analysis, Vol. 24, No. 3, 333-355.

Gibbons, Michael R.,1982, "Multivariate Test of Financial Models: A New Approach", Journal of Financial Economics, 10, 3-27.

Gultekin, Mustafa N. and N. Bulent Gultekin, 1987,"Stock Return Anomalies and Tests of the APT", Journal of Finance, 42, 1213-1224.

Hansen, Lars P. 1982, "Large Sample Properties of Generalized Method of

105

Moments Estimators." Econometrica, 50, 1029-1054.

Huberman, Gur, 1982,"Arbitrage Pricing Theory: A Simple Approach." Journal of Economic Theory, 28, 183-191.

Huberman, Gur, Shmuel Kandel and Robert Stambaugh, 1987, "Mimicking Portfolios and Exact Arbitrage Pricing", Journal of Finance, 42, 1-9.

Holtz-Eakin, Douglas , Whitney Newey and Harvey Rosen, 1988 ,"Estimating Vector Autoregressions with Panel Data", Econometrica, 56,1371-1395.

Ingersoll, Jonathan, E., Jr., 1984,"Some Results in the Theory of Arbitrage Pricing", Journal of Finance, 39, 1021-1039.

Lehmann, Bruce N. and David M. Modest, 1985, "The Empirical Foundations of the Arbitrage Pricing Theory I: The Empirical Tests". NBER Working Paper No. 1725.

Jobson, J.O., 1982, "A Multivariate Linear Regression Test for the Arbitrage Pricing Theory", Journal of Finance, 37, 1037-1042.

Mei, Jianping, 1989, "Do We Have to Know Betas ? An Autoregressive Method for Testing the APT ", Financial Research Center Working Paper #109, Princeton University.

Newey, Whitney K. and Kenneth D. West, 1987,"A Simple, Positive Semi-definite, Hetroskedasticity and Autocorrelation Consistent Covariance Matrix", Econometrica, 55, 703-708.

Reinganum, Mark, 1981, "The Arbitrage Pricing Theory: Some Empirical Results", Journal of Finance, 36, 313-321.

Roll, Richard and Stephen A. Ross, 1980, "An Empirical Investigation of the Arbitrage Pricing Theory", Journal of Finance, 35, 1073-1103.

Ross, Stephen, 1976, "The Arbitrage Theory of Capital Asset Pricing", Journal of Economic Theory, 13, 341-360.

Shanken, Jay, 1985, "Multivariate Tests of The Zero-Beta CAPM", Journal of Financial Economics, 14, 327-348.

White, Halbert ,1980,"A Heteroskedasticity-consistent Covariance Matrix Estimator and a Direct Test for Heterokedasticity", Econometrica, 48, 817-838.

White, H. and I. Domowitz, 1984,"Nonlinear Regression with Dependent Observations" , Econometrica, 52, 143-161.

White, Halbert, 1984, "Asymptotic Theory for Econometricians", New York: Academic Press.

Appendix

<u>Theorem:</u>

Suppose that:

(1) $h_i(\theta) = h(Z_i, \theta)$, where $h(Z, \theta)$ is measurable in Z for all θ, and continuously differenciable in θ for all θ in a neighborhood ω of θ^*, with probability one;

(2) (a) there is a measurable function $m(z)$ such that $sup_\omega \mid h_i(\theta) \mid\, < m(z)$ and $sup_\omega \mid h_{i\theta}(\theta) \mid\, < m(z)$, where for some finite D, $E[m(z_i)^2] < D$ for all i; (b) there are finite constant D, $\delta > 0$ and $r \geq 1$, such that for all i, $E[\mid h_i(\theta^*) \mid^{4(r+\delta)}] < D$;

(3) Z_i is a mixing sequence with $\alpha(l)$ of size $2r/(r-1)$, $r > 1$;

(4) for all i, $E[h_i(\theta^*)] = 0$, and $\sqrt{N}\,(\hat{\theta} - \theta^*)$ is bounded in probablity;

(5) the weights $w(j,M)$, $(M = 1,2,..., j = 1,...,M)$ satisfy $\mid w(j,M) \mid\, \leq C$ for finite constant C and for each j, $\lim_{M \to \infty} w(j,M) = 1$.

Then if M is chosen to be a function of $M(N)$ of sample size, N, such that $\lim_{N \to \infty} M(N) = +\infty$ and $\lim_{N \to \infty}[M(N)/T^{1/4}] = 0$, then we have:

$$\{\hat{\Omega}_0 + \sum_{j=1}^{M(N)} w(j,M(N))[\hat{\Omega}_j + \hat{\Omega}_j']\} - S_N \to 0. \qquad N \to \infty.$$

The proof can be obtained from Newey-West (1987) Theorem 2 by simply replacing the time index t with a cross section index i.

Table 1. Description of Data

===

Source: Center for Research in Security Prices
         Graduate School of Business
         University of Chicago
         Monthly Return File 1988

Selection Criteria: Firms selected must have complete information on its returns
                     and capitalization for the entire panel time span.

Variables selected   a) Return(including dividends) of the month $R_{i,t}$
   from the file: b) Month end closing price, $P_{i,t}$
                         c) Shares outstanding, $N_{i,t}$

Variables constructed: a) log capitalization, $\zeta_{i,t} = \log(P_{i,t} N_{i,t})$.

Number of securities included: 1340.

Time periods covered by the panels: 1987.1-1988.12

Number of firms in the largest 4-digit industry: 88.

===

Table 2. Test of Lag Length and Size Anomaly with Newey-West Adjustment.

$$R_{i,t} = \psi_{0t} + \sum_{j=1}^{K} \psi_{jt} R_{i,t-j} + \eta_{i,t} . \qquad i=1,...,N; \quad t=K+1,...,T. \qquad (21)$$

a) Test of Lag length

Total lags K	Q	L	DF	P
(1) K=9	18.203	_	24	0.793
(2) K=8	18.455	0.252	6	0.999
(3) K=7	18.843	0.388	6	0.998
(4) K=6	77.595	58.752	6	0.000
(4) K=5	169.834	92.239	6	0.000

$$R_{i,t} = \psi_{0t} + \sum_{j=1}^{K} \psi_{jt} R_{i,t-j} + \pi_t C_{i,t-K} + \eta_{i,t} . \qquad i=1,...,N; \quad t=K+1,...,T. \qquad (23)$$

b) Test of Size Anomaly: Ho: $\pi_t = 0$.

Total lags K	Q	L	DF	P
(1) K=9	16.872	1.331	6	0.969
(2) K=8	17.718	0.737	6	0.993
(3) K=7	18.581	0.262	6	0.999
(4) K=6	55.870	21.725	6	0.001
(4) K=5	102.068	67.766	6	0.000

Note: Equation (21) and (23) are estimated using monthly return data from 1987.1-1988.12. Returns from lag 10 to lag 18 and price from lag 10 to lag 13 are used as instruments. P gives the corresponding χ^2-square probability under which level the H_0 can be rejected.

Table 3. Test of Lag Length and Size Anomaly without Newey-West Adjustment.

$$R_{i,t} = \psi_{0t} + \sum_{j=1}^{K} \psi_{jt} R_{i,t-j} + \eta_{i,t} \ . \quad i=1,...,N; \quad t=K+1,...,T. \qquad (21)$$

a) Test of Lag length

==

Total lags K	Q	L	DF	P
(1) K=9	35.455	–	24	0.061
(2) K=8	42.461	7.006	6	0.320
(3) K=7	46.974	4.513	6	0.607
(4) K=6	64.358	17.384	6	0.007
(4) K=5	74.716	10.358	6	0.110

$$R_{i,t} = \psi_{0t} + \sum_{j=1}^{K} \psi_{jt} R_{i,t-j} + \pi_t C_{i,t-K} + \eta_{i,t} \ . \quad i=1,...,N; \quad t=K+1,...,T. \qquad (23)$$

b) Test of Size Anomaly: Ho: $\pi_t = 0$.

==

Total lags K	Q	L	DF	P
(1) K=9	26.832	8.632	6	0.195
(2) K=8	37.170	5.291	6	0.507
(3) K=7	41.251	5.723	6	0.453
(4) K=6	53.457	10.901	6	0.091
(4) K=5	60.153	14.563	6	0.023

Note: Equation (21) and (23) are estimated using monthly return data from 1987.1-1988.12. Returns from lag 10 to lag 18 and price from lag 10 to lag 13 are used as instruments. P gives the corresponding χ^2-square probability under which level the H_0 can be rejected.

Table 4. Estimates of Equation (24) for July 88-Dec. 88 (K=5)
With Newey-West Adjustment.

$$R_{i,t} = \psi_{0t} + \sum_{j=1}^{K} \psi_{jt} R_{i,t-j} + \pi_t C_{i,t-K} + \eta_{i,t} . \qquad i=1,...,N; \quad t=K+1,...,T. \qquad (23)$$

Dep.Var.	July	August	Sept.	October	November	December
Constant	0.031	0.046	-0.051	0.056	-0.049	-0.075
	(1.168)	(3.168)	(-1.882)	(1.970)	(-2.490)	(-3.080)
$R_{i,t-1}$	-0.655	-0.095	0.328	0.551	0.358	-0.475
	(-5.872)	(-0.665)	(1.193)	(4.893)	(2.182)	(-3.729)
$R_{i,t-2}$	0.001	-0.004	0.006	-0.002	0.002	0.004
	(0.544)	(-4.442)	(3.277)	(-1.057)	(1.396)	(1.985)
$R_{i,t-3}$	0.357	-0.066	-0.208	0.490	0.104	-0.636
	(2.274)	(-0.911)	(-0.822)	(2.650)	(1.282)	(-3.308)
$R_{i,t-4}$	-0.080	0.504	0.076	-0.131	-0.077	0.848
	(-0.567)	(4.442)	(0.768)	(-0.630)	(-0.685)	(5.306)
$R_{i,t-5}$	0.182	--0.253	0.078	-0.532	0.074	-0.609
	(2.254)	(-2.376)	(0.413)	(-4.349)	(0.443)	(-2.920)
$C_{i,t-5}$	-0.091	-0.150	0.047	-0.374	-0.222	0.545
	(-0.936)	(-1.630)	(0.310)	(-1.743)	(-1.818)	(3.047)

Note: Equation (23) are estimated using monthly return data from 1987.1-1988.12.
Returns from lag 10 to lag 18 and price from lag 10 to lag 13 are used as
instruments. T-statistics are given in parentheses.

Table 5. Estimates of Equation (24) for July 88-Dec. 88 (K=5)
Without Newey-West Adjustment.

$$R_{i,t} = \psi_{0t} + \sum_{j=1}^{K} \psi_{jt} R_{i,t-j} + \pi_t C_{i,t-K} + \eta_{i,t} . \qquad i=1,\dots,N; \quad t=K+1,\dots,T. \qquad (23)$$

Dep.Var.	July	August	Sept.	October	November	December
Constant	-0.005	0.055	-0.053	-0.100	-0.076	-0.040
	(-0.130)	(1.892)	(-1.058)	(-2.062)	(-2.189)	(-0.775)
$R_{i,t-1}$	-0.542	0.222	-0.005	-0.078	0.363	-0.190
	(-2.449)	(0.817)	(-0.009)	(-0.340)	(1.179)	(-0.677)
$R_{i,t-2}$	0.002	-0.005	0.006	0.010	0.003	0.003
	(0.884)	(-2.513)	(1.450)	(2.701)	(1.176)	(0.578)
$R_{i,t-3}$	0.029	0.010	-0.297	1.230	0.118	-0.902
	(0.107)	(0.078)	(-0.545)	(3.398)	(0.596)	(-2.448)
$R_{i,t-4}$	0.232	0.758	0.085	-0.396	0.191	0.676
	(0.703)	(3.502)	(0.397)	(-0.877)	(0.791)	(2.320)
$R_{i,t-5}$	0.075	--0.288	0.439	-0.142	0.016	-0.462
	(0.441)	(-1.558)	(0.998)	(-0.540)	(0.061)	(-1.295)
$C_{i,t-5}$	-0.153	-0.068	0.136	-0.706	0.005	0.009
	(-0.739)	(-0.453)	(0.386)	(-1.698)	(0.020)	(0.028)

Note: Equation (23) are estimated using monthly return data from 1987.1-1988.12.
Returns from lag 10 to lag 18 and price from lag 10 to lag 13 are used as
instruments. T-statistics are given in parentheses.